Big Fat Cat AND THE GHOST AVENUE

Takahiko Mukoyama
Tetsuo Takashima
with studio ET CETERA

GENTOSHA

はじめに

この本をパラパラとめくって、
先のページをご覧になった方は驚いていると思います。
別の本を買ってしまったと思うかもしれませんが、
これはまちがいなく BFC BOOKS の三冊目です。

まだ気がついていないみなさまには、改めてお知らせします。
今回の『ビッグ・ファット・キャットとゴースト・アベニュー』は
今までとはちょっとちがいます。
どこがちがうかって？

それはまだ秘密です。

でも、ひとつだけ頭に入れておいてください。
今回の物語は多少読めないところがあっても、
気にせず、とばして、どんどん先へ進んでください。
今回はそういう回です。
詳しくはまた解説で！

これまでのあらすじ

　ある冬の寒い日、お人よしのパイ職人エド・ウィッシュボーンは一夜にして家と仕事を失い、途方に暮れて街へ出た。手元に残ったのは、エドの気持ちなどどこ吹く風の太った猫が一匹だけ。ハイウェイ脇を町はずれのモーテルへと向かっていたエドは、猫にサンドイッチを奪われたり、通りがかったリムジンに泥水をかけられたりして、いよいよどん底の気分になっていく。

　しかし、ニュー・エヴァーヴィル・モールの看板に「空き店舗あり」の文字を目にしたエドは、いつの間にかニュー・モールの入り口に立っていた。そしてモール内のフードコートで実際の空き店舗を目にすると、いちかばちかオーナーの部屋を訪れてみようと決心する。

　オーナーの部屋は立派なたたずまいで、ボロボロのいでたちのエドはただでさえ萎縮してしまうが、さらにタイミングの悪いことに、ちょうど空き店舗の件で先客が来ているところだった。先ほどエドに泥水をかけていったリムジンの青年、ジェレミー・ライトフット・ジュニアである。怖そうなボディーガードを引き連れたジェレミーは、町一番の権力者の御曹司で、新進のチェーン店「ゾンビ・パイ」の仕掛け人でもあった。

　思わずあきらめかけたエドだったが、オーナーはエドの純粋な思いに興味を持ち、ジェレミーの反論をはねのけて、二つある空き店舗のうち、小さい方をエドに任せてもよいと言い出した。条件はただひとつ、今日の閉店時間までに最初の家賃を払うこと。驚きから我に返ったエドは閉店まであと一時間と知り、大急ぎでニュー・モールから交差点を隔てた銀行へと急ぐ。

　夢がかなうかもしれないという興奮と緊張を抱えて、何度も転びそうになりながら、エドは必死に走った。今まで何度となく人生に遅れてきたエドは、今回もまた遅れてしまうのではないかと不安を感じていた。それでも無事にお金を下ろして、モールへ戻ってきたその時――すっかりおなかをすかせた猫がエドに飛びついてくる。思わず転んでしまったところに、不審なリムジンが猛スピードで近づき、地面に落ちた鞄をひったくって行ってしまった。

　エドは車にはねられ、駐車場に転がった。必死に起き上がった時にはお金だけでなく、猫までが姿を消していた。遠のく意識の中、エドは猫を呼ぶが、返事は返ってこなかった……。

Big Fat Cat and the Ghost Avenue

光があたれば、影ができます。
みんなが光の中にいることができればいいのですが、
影の中にしか居場所のない人たちもたくさんいます。

エドは自分がずっと光のあたる場所で
生きてきたことを知りませんでした。
そして、光の届かない場所にも
懸命に生きている人たちがいることを。

今、光と影が、時間に忘れられた通りで出会おうとしています。
そこは世界からこぼれ落ちた者たちの集うところ……
幽霊の街、ゴースト・アベニューへようこそ！

Something was wrong.

The owner knew this before he got the call. Because the young man, Ed Wishbone, had not returned to the office. Maybe Ed Wishbone had been lying about the amount of money he had. Or maybe he had just changed his mind and walked away. Young people are sometimes like that, especially nowadays.

But the owner knew better. He knew an honest man when he saw one. Ed Wishbone was not a very sharp person, but he was definitely not a liar. And the fact that Jeremy Lightfoot's bodyguard stepped out of his office after Ed was not comforting at all.

So when the clinic called, the owner was not really surprised. He just rushed over there.

The clinic was at the west end of the mall, along a narrow corridor between a hobby shop and a greeting card store. Inside the clinic, the owner found a nurse standing in front of the door to the examining rooms.

"Which room?" the owner asked.

"The one at the end of the hallway."

"What happened to him?"

"He was hit by a car. His wounds are minor but we're worried about his head. He hit it pretty hard on the asphalt. We want to send him to the city hospital, but he won't go."

"Why not?"

"I'm not sure. He may be confused from the shock. Said something about looking for a cat. He wanted to leave but we stopped him. He shouldn't even get out of bed yet."

The owner frowned and knocked on the door. When there was no answer, he opened it. He was greeted by an ice-cold gust of wind.

"What the...? Mr. Wishbone?"

Wind was blowing in from an open window. The curtains were flapping against the walls madly. The owner ran to the window and poked his head out.

"Mr. Wishbone!?"

The November cold filled the darkness of the parking lot. The only light came from the half moon above. There was no sign of anyone anywhere.

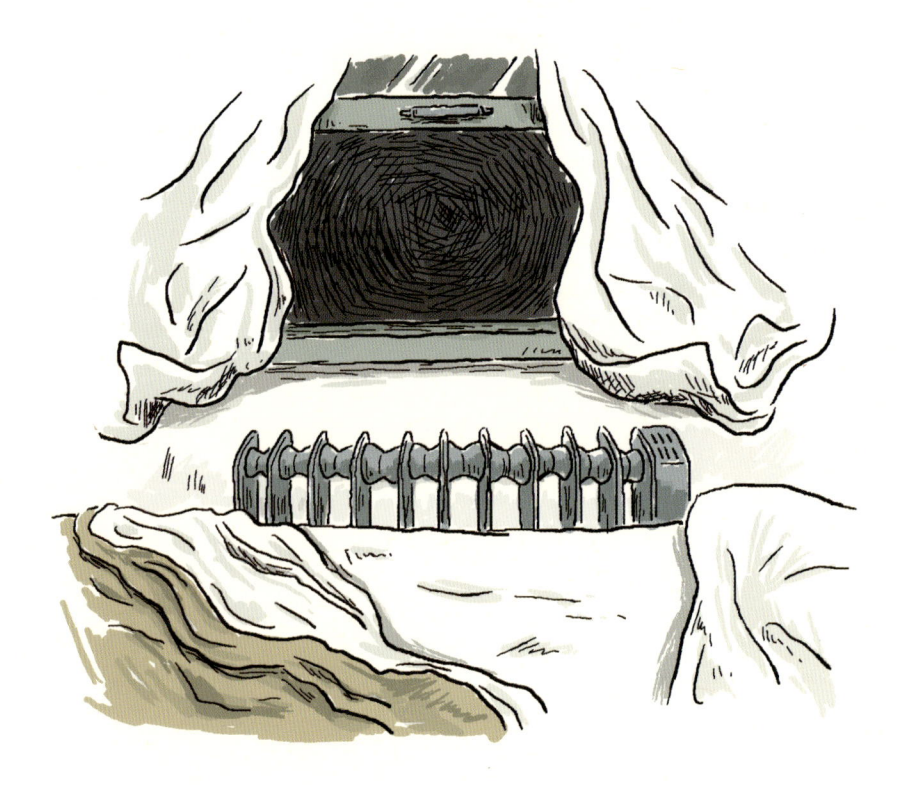

"Oh my God..."

I was late...

I was late again...
(But it wasn't my fault!)

I'm cold... got to find the cat... so cold...
(*Where am I?*)

I'm a failure. I've always been a failure.
(*It was the cat's fault!*)

Got to find the cat...
(*so cold... so cold... so...*)

cold...

"Son, you're gonna freeze to death if you sleep here," a voice said. It was a soft voice.

Ed moaned. He was cold. His cheek was lying on something hard.

"Son, you really better wake up."

Ed stirred and opened his eyes. His memory was a blur. He didn't know where or when he was.

An old man was standing over him. The man had a long white beard, very old skin, and eyes that reminded Ed of Santa Claus. But it was a little too early for Santa, and Santa definitely didn't dress like this.

"Son, I don't know what the heck you're doing here, but you better wake up if you don't wanna become a damn Popsicle."

The old man moved slowly, pushing a baby stroller filled with books, magazines, and newspapers. One of the wheels of the stroller was missing. It had been replaced with the lid of a pot.

Ed got up with difficulty. He was lying in a dark, dirty street. The street was lined on both sides with buildings that had been closed for a long time. It was quiet except for the rattle of the old man's stroller.

"Where am I?" Ed said in a weak voice. His head was hurting like crazy.

"You don't know where you are?"

"I think... I... I'm lost..."

"Damn right you are. Everyone who comes here is lost. Pretty badly lost, as a matter of fact."

Ed looked around again. The moon overhead cast shadows into every corner. A gust of wind blew down the street.

Ed just wanted to sleep. He didn't want to walk anymore. He had never been so tired in his whole life.

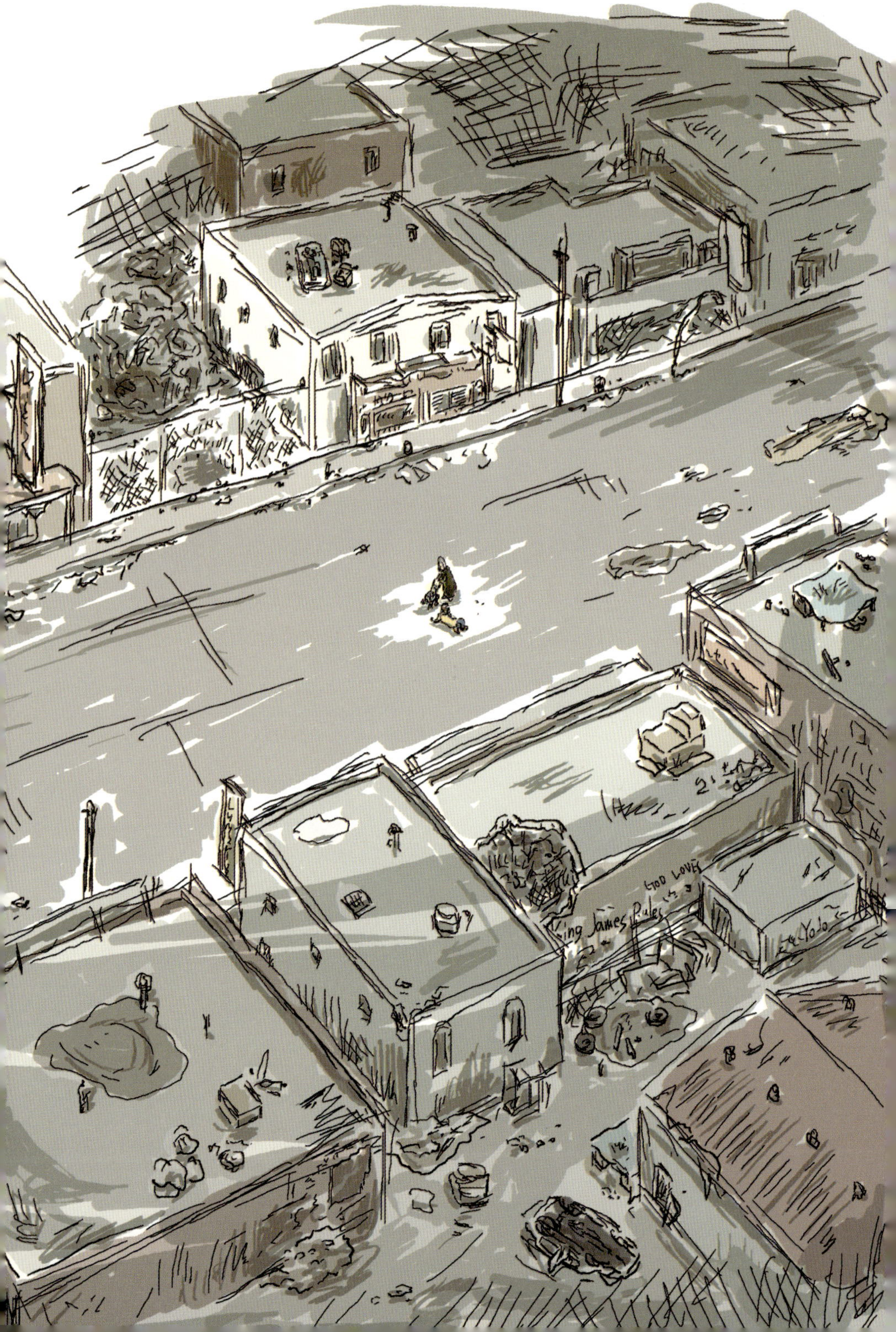
GOD LOVES
ing James Rules
YoJo

The old man walked over to a giant pile of junk by the side of the road. The pile was made of stuff that had been thrown away when the street was still a part of the town.

"People have forgotten about this place. They call it 'Ghost Avenue' now. We're just ghosts to them."

The old man picked a long piece of cloth that had probably been a curtain some decades ago. He turned around to Ed and smiled.

"We call it 'Treasure Island'."

Ed blinked. His blurry mind figured out that he was somewhere on the northwest side of town, near the old mines. The area had been busy during the twenties and thirties because of the mining business. The barber from the shop next to Pie Heaven had told him that there used to be a beautiful old cinema here.

"Folks around here call me Willy. Professor Willy. Because I'm the only one who can read," the old man said.

He handed Ed the long piece of cloth. Ed took it reluctantly and wrapped it around himself. It smelled bad.

"I... I'm Ed," he managed to say.

The light of the moon played with the shadows. It was as if the street was alive.

"Nice to meet you, Ed. Now follow me," Willy said, and started down the street.

Ed followed Willy slowly, walking deeper into the darkness of the street.

17

Meanwhile, in another part of town...

CLUNK

BAM!

Oof!
Oo...

And back in Ghost Avenue...

"Here we are," Willy said, stopping in front of a unique two-story structure. Ed looked up at the building in wonder. It was a great big building.

The Old Everville Cinema really was beautiful. The barber had not been kidding. He had not been kidding about the 'old' part either. But the cinema still remained beautiful in a strange sort of way.

"This used to be a great theater back in the fifties, you know. Big screen, great flicks, buttered popcorn... But that was a long time ago. Now it's our home," Willy said as he pushed open the doors of the once-glamorous theater.

Inside, the theater lobby was ruined. The refreshment stand, the ticket booth, and the waiting area had been torn down, and everything had been replaced with piles of cardboard and miscellaneous junk. A few people were sitting there in the dark. The only light inside was a lantern hung from the remains of a chandelier.

A man rummaging through a pile of soda cans looked up and grinned at Ed.

"That's Frank," Willy said as he pushed his stroller through the mess. "He won't hurt you. Nice guy. Stinks, but a nice guy anyway."

"Howdy," Frank said to Ed, raising his hand awkwardly. He had no teeth. Ed just kept walking.

Willy walked across the lobby to a set of swinging doors that were hidden behind a broken vending machine. Ed followed cautiously, glancing around the whole time.

The main part of the theater was better preserved than the lobby, except for one major difference. There was a big hole in the ceiling. The blue half moon shined through the hole, providing a soft light. There was also a warm red glow from a small campfire that was burning directly underneath the hole.

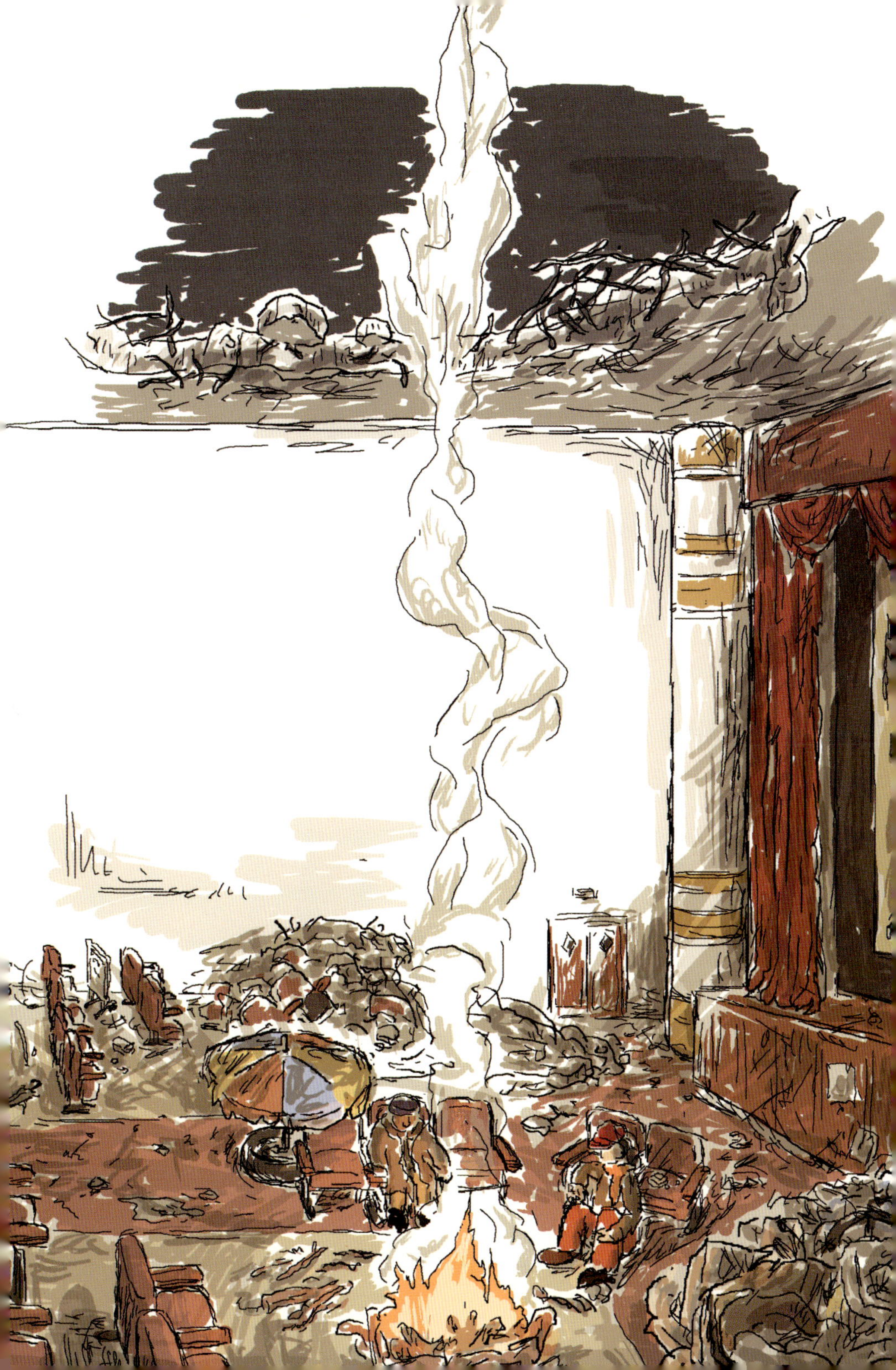

"Here. Use them."

Willy pointed to a row of seats near the campfire. Ed sat down. He found the seats very mushy, but he didn't care. The seats were much better than the cold street outside.

"Well, you've met Frank, and that's George and Beejees. Louie's in that box over there, I don't know where Paddy is, but Marv's probably in the basement. He almost never comes out."

Ed nodded.

"What do you do for a living, Ed?" Willy asked as he tossed a few crumpled-up pieces of newspaper into the fire.

"I bake... I used to bake pies," Ed said, staring into the burning fire.

"That's a nice job."

"I lost my shop yesterday. I'm not a baker anymore."

"Sure you are. You're just a baker without a shop."

"Not just my shop. I lost my house, my savings[貯金], my bag, my whole life... all I have left is this."

Ed took his rolling pin out of his coat pocket. Somebody had found it lying near him in the parking lot of the New Mall. It always seemed to survive[生存する] somehow. Ed tossed it on the ground.

It rolled straight toward the fire. It would have burned up if Willy hadn't reached out and grabbed it.

"Don't. This is important to you."

"No," Ed said. "I'm really not much of a baker. I just like baking pies. I was a mediocre[平凡な] salesman until last year. I quit my job, thinking I could become a pie baker because my mom used to bake great pies. She won a lot of contests. I thought maybe I was like her. But I wasn't. Stupid[まぬけ]."

Willy stood by the fire, listening with a faint[かすかな] smile on his face. It was a smile worn[磨耗した] by time and hardened[固くなった], almost petrified[化石化する], by the burdens[重荷] of life.

Ed continued to speak, the light of the fire playing on his face.

"Mom always told me that life was like a blueberry pie. Sometimes it's sour but most of the time it's sweet. She said the most wonderful thing in life was to eat a good, warm slice of pie."

A tear formed[形作る] at the corner of Ed's eye and rolled down his cheek.

27

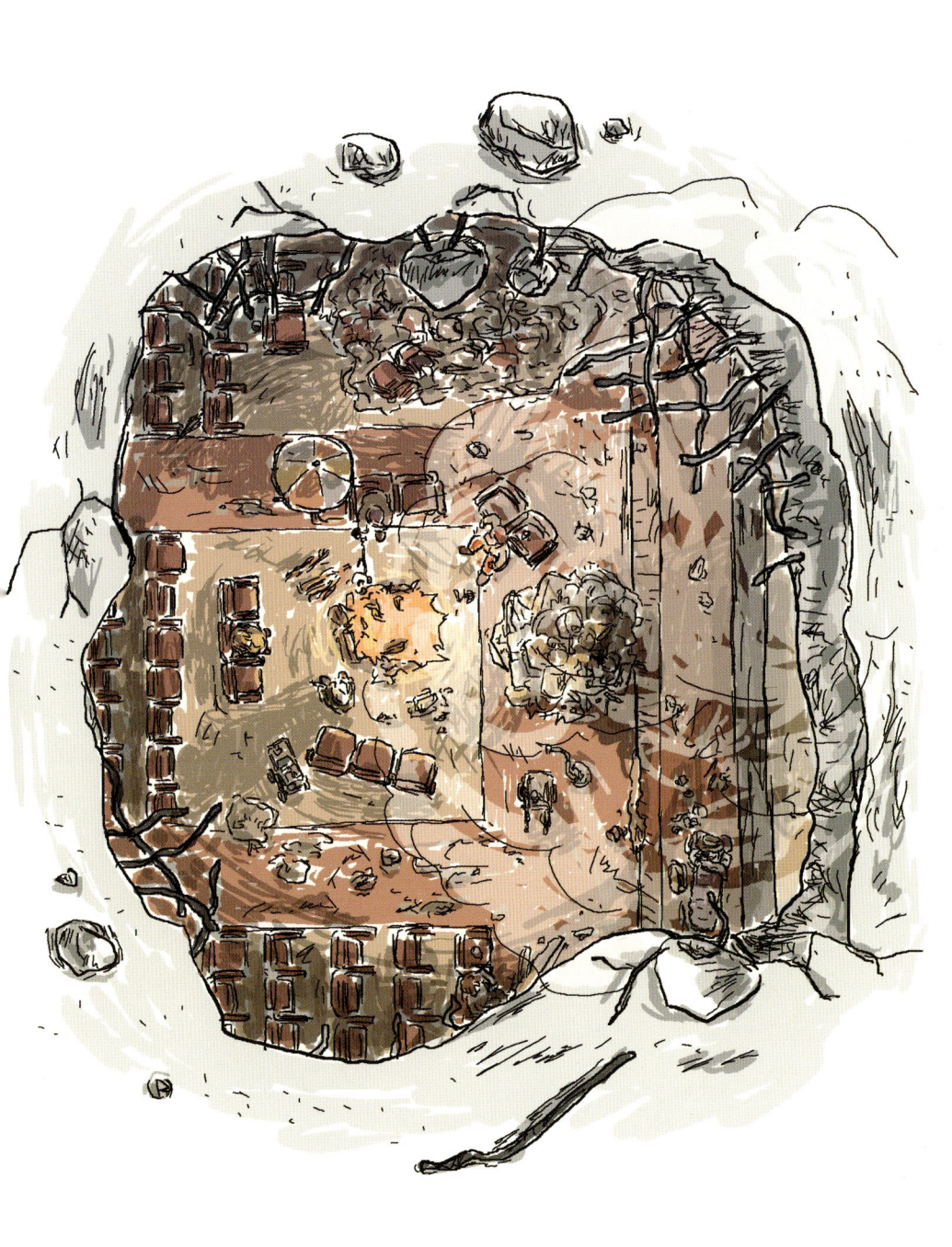

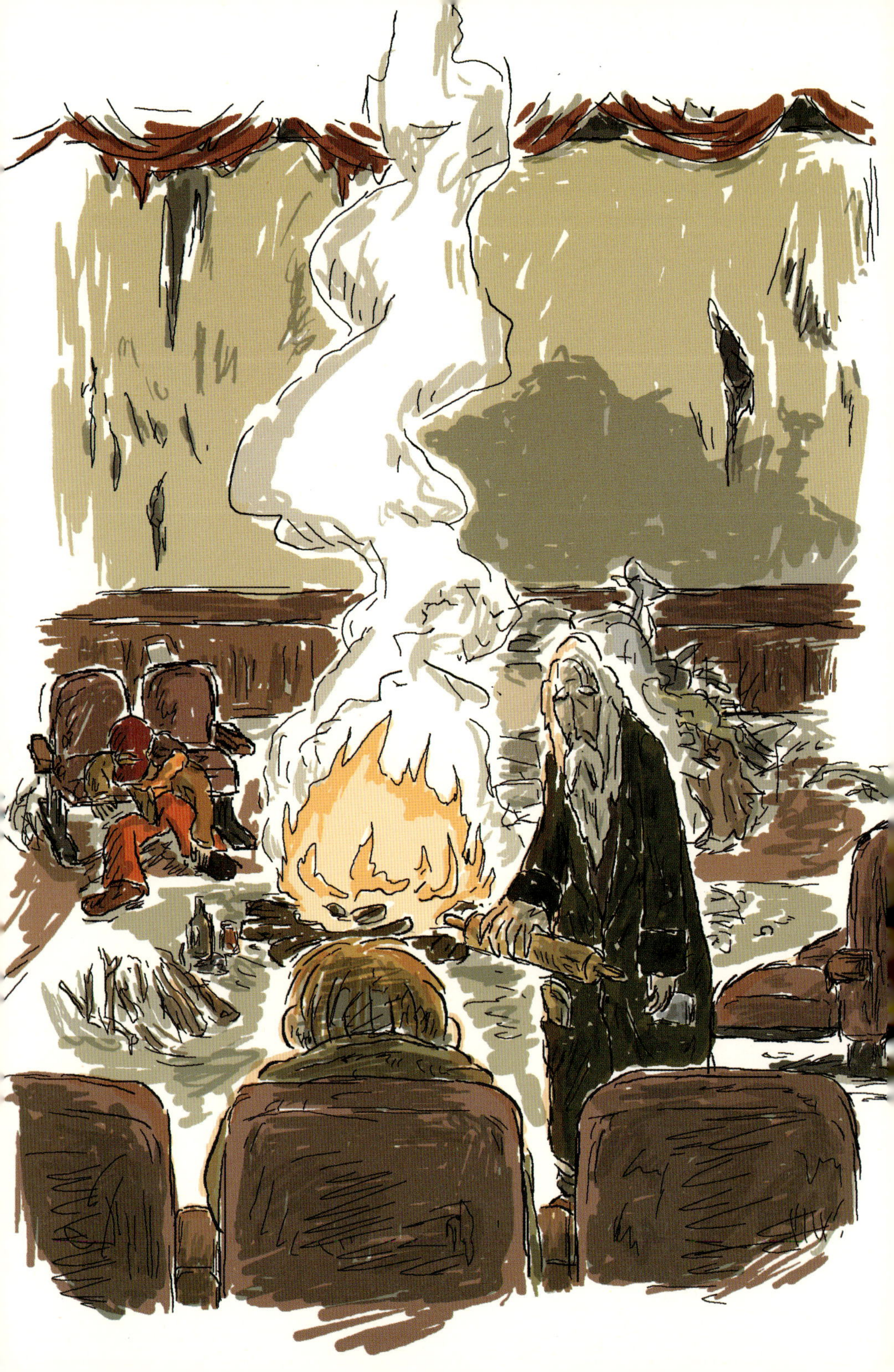

"But she was wrong, you know. She died of a heart attack when I was in high school. From overwork. My father had left us the year before, and she'd had to work two jobs to raise me. One day when I came home from school, there was a slice of warm blueberry pie on the table. She was sitting in front of the oven, waiting for the pie to cool. But... she wasn't breathing. No last words. I never even said 'thank you' to her. I was too late. I'm always too damn late."

Willy walked up to Ed and held the rolling pin out to him. Ed shook his head, tears streaming down his face.

"No. I'm not going to bake any more pies. Life isn't a blueberry pie. A child can see that. It's... it's... more like a mustard pie."

"Look, Ed. You're going to get a good night's sleep, and then in the morning, you're going to go back to your life. You are not one of us. You have a life. Go back to it."

"You don't understand. I can't bake pies like my mother. I don't have it in me. I was only pretending I could."

"That's because you have no idea what a pie is really made of."

"Sure I do. I use the same things my mother did. I even use the same brand of flour. It doesn't make any difference."

"You had a great mom. She understood life well. She knew why pies were important. That's why she was a great baker."

"Pies are just pies. They're not important."

    A long silent moment passed. Ed looked away while Willy
tended the fire. The crackling sounds of the fire eating into the
wood filled the air. Finally, Willy spoke. His voice was slow and
calm.

    "Most of us haven't had a slice of pie in years, Ed."

    Ed stopped wiping his tears. Still wearing that faint and
petrified smile, Willy continued, "Take Frank for example. He's
been here for more than ten years now. He's probably forgotten
what a pie looks like."

Willy gestured toward Frank, who was now near the campfire, looking for something in another big pile of junk.

"Why doesn't he just buy one?" Ed said with a rather guilty look on his face. "I mean, he could get a job, couldn't he? A pie is just a buck or so. Frank chose to be here... just like me. Bad luck, but it's probably his own fault. Anybody can buy a piece of pie. You just need to go out and..."

At that moment, Frank moved toward the fire. Ed suddenly noticed that he had no legs.

The tears came back all at once. Ed's face turned red and he covered his mouth with his hand. The tears streamed over his hand.

"I'm... I'm sorry. I didn't mean... oh no... I'm... I'm so sorry. I'm so confused... I'm really, really sorry..."

"No harm done, Ed," Willy said. "Frank was born on the street. Never knew his parents... A car hit him when he was twenty. Three hospitals refused to treat him and he ended up here."

The soft light of the moon enveloped the theater in its warm glow. The smoke from the campfire rose through the hole in the ceiling, up toward the sky, where it scattered among the clouds. The whole theater seemed like a gentle shelter for life.

"Ed... most of us here will die without eating another piece of pie... and we're the luckier ones. Some people never have the chance to eat pie. Not once in their lives. Some people have never had anything sweet, not in their mouths or in their hearts. For those people, Ed, life isn't a blueberry pie or a mustard pie. Life is just hell."

Willy put the rolling pin down on the seat beside Ed and turned toward the campfire again.

"Sleep, Ed. Then go back. Bake more pies."

And it was a long night. The longest night of Ed's life. He was as tired as possible, but he still could not sleep.

He watched the campfire burn down.

He watched the moon shining in the sky.

And he watched the "ghosts" of Everville sleeping in their beds of garbage. Garbage that he might have thrown away.

He thought about all the pies he had baked. He thought even more about the many pies he had thrown away.

He thought of his mother.

He thought of his mother a lot that night.

Life is like a blueberry pie, Eddie. Sometimes it's sour, but most of the time, it's sweet.

For the first time in ten years, Ed remembered that there was something after those words. Perhaps the most important part which he had forgotten a long time ago.

And you know what, Eddie? It's always sweet if you eat it with the people you love.

Ed cried himself to sleep, and in the morning, he knew what he had to do.

When Willy woke up that morning, he couldn't believe what he smelled. It was the smell of fresh-baked pie. It was something he hadn't smelled for a long, long time. Willy got up and found his fellow ghosts standing around the campfire with Ed.

Ed was slicing up an apple pie.

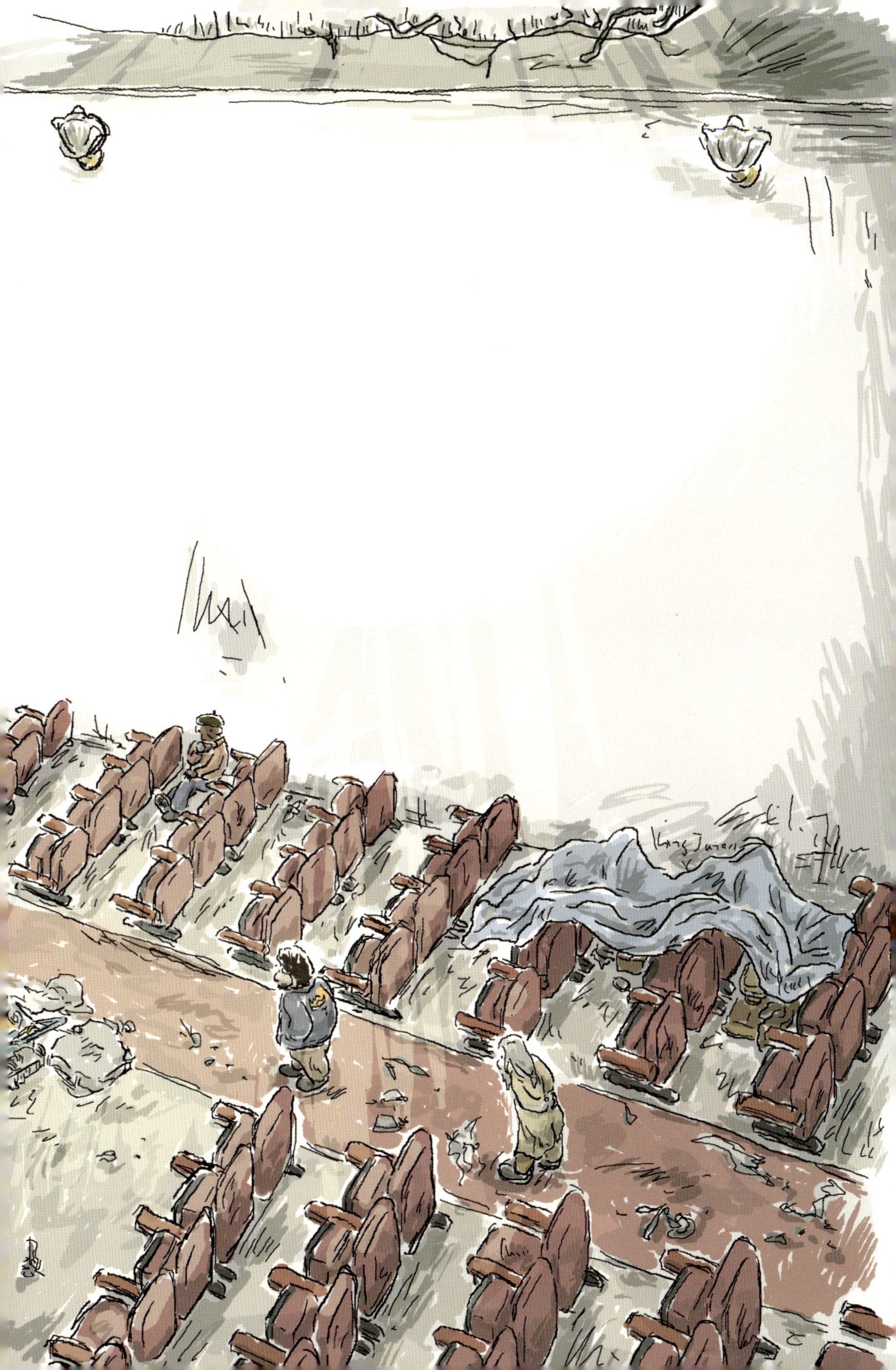

"I'll be darned," Willy mumbled, his eyes wide with astonishment.

A metal container was hanging over the campfire, and more pies were baking inside of it. Ed saw Willy and spoke to him with a smile.

"I only had enough money for apple jam, so I guess it's not a genuine apple pie. And the crust is just graham crackers. But I did the best I could. I saved you a big piece. Here."

Willy took the slice of apple pie from Ed. It was on a piece of wax paper. No fork, no napkin, but it was really apple pie.

"You were right. I guess I am a baker after all," Ed said.

Willy bit into the pie. It was sweet. It smelled of a long time ago.

"Thank you," Willy said with a big smile.

Ed smiled back and said, "I'm going to get some more wax paper."

"Sure. Oh, Paddy's probably out in front of the theater sweeping. Please give him a slice too."

"Okay, I'll look for him," Ed said, and stepped out of the theater.

But Paddy wasn't there.

Instead, Ed saw a big black man standing by the side of Ghost Avenue. The man's eyes were searching for something. Ed froze, the slice of apple pie held in his hand. He recognized the man from somewhere. The man looked like the bodyguard who had been standing behind the rich man at the New Mall's office. He also looked a lot like the man who had grabbed his bag.

At that moment, the man's eyes met Ed's eyes, and Ed suddenly knew what the man had been searching for.

Because the man had just found it.

Ed started to turn around, but it was too late. The man seized Ed from behind and slammed him against the outside wall of the theater.

"No words," the man whispered to Ed as he held him against the wall.

Completely terrified, Ed was unable to speak anyway.

"Understand?" the man whispered again.

Ed nodded desperately, although he could not understand what was happening at all. He could barely breathe.

The giant black man stuffed a piece of paper in Ed's mouth and said just two more words.

"Sign it."

Ed nodded at once. It was the only thing he could do.

The man let him go. Ed dropped to his knees on the ground, the pie falling from his hand. The man tossed a pen at Ed, and then started walking back to the limousine. Shaking all over, Ed picked up the pen and started signing his name. He couldn't think. He was too scared.

Before he finished signing his name, the sound of the limousine door rang in his ear. Ed raised his eyes from the ground and saw something that made his blood run cold.

The man was holding Ed's bag.

And something was stuffed inside.
Something very still.
Something shaped like a big, fat cat.

The man came back, and set the bag down in front of Ed. Then the man picked up the paper. He checked the signature quickly, and without even a glance at Ed, started back to the limousine.

Ed's heart was bouncing in his chest. He had the urge to throw up but he pushed it back. He remembered thinking that all of his problems were the cat's fault.

"Oh, cat... I'm sorry... I'm so sorry..."

Ed slowly pulled the zipper of the bag open.

"AAAGGGGGHHHHHH!!"

Ed shouted as a very frustrated cat popped out of the bag with a snarl and scratched his face. The cat leaped aside, and almost immediately noticed the piece of pie on the ground. The cat took a giant stretch, and with the grace that only cats possess, approached the pie and started to devour it.

A smile of relief appeared on Ed's face, as he sat down on the sidewalk weakly. The limousine had already driven away. Ed leaned against the wall of the theater and let out a deep breath. He still couldn't understand what that had been all about. It was probably something about the vacant space in the mall, but he didn't care anymore. He was just glad that it was over.

The cat finished the piece of pie and looked up at Ed for more. It seemed dissatisfied, maybe because the pie was not blueberry.

"You understand a lot more than you seem to, don't you, cat?" Ed asked. A weak but sincere smile spread across his face.

"Blueberry pie is the only pie I still make from my mom's original recipe."

Ed looked into the cat's eyes. The cat looked back. It was a weird but pleasant moment, there on the sidewalk of a forgotten town. One cat and its owner, just staring at each other awkwardly.

Then, after a long silent moment, the cat burped.

"Ugh! That's horrible," Ed laughed.

The cat made an annoyed face and started to look for somewhere warm to take a nap. It still seemed hungry. Ed's laughter echoed down the wide, empty road of Ghost Avenue, up and down, over and below, and on into the first glimpse of the day ahead.

Ed Wishbone knew that the rest of his life had begun.

and the story continues...

『ビッグ・ファット・キャットとゴースト・アベニュー』をもっと読み込む

これまでこのコーナーでは、本文の解説をしてきました。
前作『ビッグ・ファット・キャット、街へ行く』には
仕上げの意味を込めて、特に細かい解説を収録しました。
でも、もう十分だと思います。

これ以上細かい内容に入ってしまうと、
せっかく面白くなりかけてきた英語を
またつまらないものにしてしまう危険性があります。
「分かってきた」「もうちょっとで分かりそうな気がする」
というところがちょうどいい地点で、
「もう少し」やると、かえって行きすぎになり、
英語が再び複雑なものに思えてきます。

でも、解説することはまだあります。
あまり見たことのない解説かもしれませんが、
本を読む上では大切なことばかりです。

BFC BOOKS が贈る「もうひとつの解説」へようこそ！

文章は読まなくても機能する

すでにお気づきの方も多いかと思いますが、今回の『ビッグ・ファット・キャットとゴースト・アベニュー』は前の二作に比べて、より本格的な物語となっています。文字の多いページを発見して、英語でこんなに読めないのではないかと心配になった方も多いと思います。

でも、だいじょうぶです。心配する必要はありません。というのも、難しくて読めないところにあたったら、とばしてしまえばいいからです。

「それじゃ、物語をちゃんと読んだことにならないのでは……？」と、不安に感じる方もいるかもしれません。でも、日本語ならそうしてはいませんか？　英語だからといって、特別視する必要はありません。「とばして読む」というのはある種の技術です。そして、それは悪いことではありません。とばしても、物語は十分楽しむことができるからです。むしろ、とばすべきだとさえ言えるかもしれません。

今からその理由を説明しましょう。

これは今回の『ビッグ・ファット・キャットとゴースト・アベニュー』の冒頭のページです。このページの文章を二つの色に塗り分けてみました。

p.4
Something was wrong.
　The owner knew this before he got the call. Because the young man, Ed Wishbone, had not returned to the office. Maybe Ed Wishbone had been lying about the amount of money he had. Or maybe he had just changed his mind and walked away. Young people are sometimes like that, especially nowadays.
　But the owner knew better. He knew an honest man when he saw one. Ed Wishbone was not a very sharp person, but he was definitely

not a liar. And the fact that Jeremy Lightfoot's bodyguard stepped out of his office after Ed was not comforting at all.
　So when the clinic called, the owner was not really surprised. He just rushed over there.

　まず注目してほしいのは、薄い赤色に塗られたところです。いちばん多くて、しかも中心にあるので重要な部分に見えますが、実はそうでもありません。薄い赤色に塗られているところは、本来必要のないところです。
　小説はどの言語で書かれていても、8〜9割の文章は、物語上では取り立てて必要のないものです。これらの文章をフル理解すればさらに物語が面白くなりますが、分からなくても話は十分に楽しむことができます。いわば、飾りのようなものです。お皿の模様やカーテンの柄と同じで、あればきれいですが、なくても機能は変わりません。この飾りの部分に何を書くか、そしてどう書くかが、それぞれの作家の個性だと言えるかもしれません。
　でも、実際に物語を進める「動力源」となるのはわずかな文章だけです。ここでは濃い赤色の文が「動力源」の文章です。読む時はこの部分にだけは注意が必要です。といっても、すべてを理解しなくてもかまいません。今まで何度も繰り返してきましたが、あくまで文章で大事なのは箱と矢印（またはイコール）の部分だけで、付録の部分は分からなくてもだいじょうぶです。

　なぜ小説にはそんなに無駄な部分が多いのかというと、それは小説は映画や音楽とちがって、物語の中の「時間」をコントロールできないメディアだからです。一見無駄な文章や表現は、基本的にそこに「間」がほしいために入れられています。だから、極端なことを言えば、読めなくてもいいのかもしれません。
　たとえばこういうシーンがあったとします。

Jeremy Lightfoot Jr.'s Words of Wisdom

"Money is not important. A lot of money is."

— Jery Lightfoot Jr.

【例1】
　エドはドアを開けるのをためらった。彼の手は汗で濡れていた。背中がひどく緊張している。この奥についに探し求めていた答えがあるのだ。エドは思い切ってドアを開けた。

　薄い赤の部分をまるまる消してしまっても、エドの動作や、物語の進行が変わるわけではありません。エドがドアを開けるまでの時間の経過を示す「間」として、エドの心の中の描写が入っているだけです。では、代わりにその「間」のところに音楽の休符を入れてみましょう。読む時に、休符の所も文字として目で追ってみてください。

【例2】
　エドはドアを開けるのをためらった。♪♪♪♪♪♪♪♪♪♪♪♪♪♪♪♪♪♪♪♪♪♪♪♪♪♪♪エドは思い切ってドアを開けた。

　休符の上を目で追ってから最後の文を読むと、例1の文章を読んだのとそんなに大きく感じが変わらないことが分かります。このような「間」を作る文は、たとえ文そのものが理解できなくても、文字の上に目を通していくだけで十分機能を果たします。
　これが「とばす」という技術の正体です。

　先ほどの本文4ページでは、真ん中のオーナーの思考（薄い赤に塗ってある部分）は、主にオーナーが部屋から医務室まで歩いている「間」を表現するために入っています。もちろんただの「間」ではつまらないので、オーナーのエドに対する気持ちを補足したり、前作の舞台裏を少し明かしたりもしていますが、それらはおまけのようなものです。

THE EVERVILLE TRAVELER'S HANDBOOK
エヴァーヴィル・トラベラーズ・ハンドブック
ロドリー・ハドソン 著　　向山貴彦 訳

基本的には速足で医務室へ歩いている効果を生むのが最大の役割です。

実際に読めないと困ってしまう「動力源」となっているところはわずかです。試しに挿絵を見ながら、濃い赤の部分だけを読んでみてください。この時、薄い赤のところを目で追って、オーナーが何かぶつぶつつぶやいているような感じを想像すれば、実際にこのページを読んだのとそれほど読後感が変わらないのではないでしょうか。

小説の持つこういった性質を知っておくと、もっと気軽に物語が楽しめます。本を読み慣れている人は、無意識にこの「とばす」作業をしています。こうすることで、分からないところで詰まってリズムを崩し、せっかく盛り上がってきたストーリーを止めることなく、作者の意図している速度も失わずにすみます。

どんなに面白い四コママンガでも、一コマずつ、一時間おきに見たらつまらなくなってしまいます。小説も同様です。楽しみの半分は緻密に計画された「時間の進行」です。最初に読む時はなるべく辞書を引かずに、その「間」を楽しむことをお勧めするのはこのためです。

もちろん辞書を引いてはいけないということはありません。気になる単語があったらどんどん引いてください。ただし、面倒だと感じない範囲にしておくことがコツです。楽しむために本を読んでいるのですから、たとえ英語の本でも、それが苦痛になるなら本末転倒です。万が一、本をちゃんと読み終えることができなかったら、その理由は次の二つのどちらかです。その本が……

1．今の難易度にあっていない。
もしくは、
2．夢中になれない本だった。

PROFILE 〜プロフィール〜
人口・・・・・・・8241人
シンボルマーク・・・鳥と湖
名物・・・・・・・ナマズ料理　コーヒーロール
交通・・・・・・・市内循環バス、長距離バス、ローデン空港までの往復シャトルバス

どちらにしても、読者の責任ではありません。こういう場合は気にせず、また別の本を探してみてください。

ひととおり読み終えたら、二回目以降はその小説の進む速度を知っているわけですから、途中で邪魔が入っても、自分で感覚を調整することができます。そうなると、今度は辞書やインターネットを自由に使って、細かい仕掛けや伏線を読み取っていけば、また別の楽しみ方ができます。いい物語は一回目と二回目でちがう楽しさを用意してくれています。いろいろ探してみないと損かもしれません。

セリフについて

次に本文 5 ページの文章を見てみましょう。ここは 4 ページとは雰囲気も仕組みも少し異なるページです。薄い赤の文はここでもあまり必要のない文です

p.5
The clinic was at the west end of the mall, along a narrow corridor between a hobby shop and a greeting card store. Inside the clinic, the owner found a nurse standing in front of the door to the examining rooms.
"Which room?" the owner asked.
"The one at the end of the hallway."
"What happened to him?"
"He was hit by a car. His wounds are minor but we're worried about his head. He hit it pretty hard on the asphalt. We want to send him to the city hospital, but he won't go."
"Why not?"
"I'm not sure. He may be confused from the shock. Said something about looking for a cat. He wanted to leave but we stopped him. He shouldn't even get out of bed yet."

HISTORY　〜歴史〜
1800年代の終わりから1900年代の初めにかけて、スパイグラス山脈で金が出るという噂が流れ、たくさんの人々が一攫千金を夢見てこの未開の地に集まった。金の運搬のために鉄道が開通する計画が持ち上がり、中継基地として栄えることを当て込んだ商人たちが次々に現在のエヴリー湖周辺に宿屋や食事処を開いたことで、小さな村落が形成された。

一目で分かるとおり、ほとんどが濃い赤の文です。「間」となる薄い赤の文がわずかしかありません。これはこのページがほとんど「動き」と「セリフ」で構成されているスピーディーなシーンだからです。

　第一作の『ビッグ・ファット・キャットとマスタード・パイ』を同じやり方で色分けしたとしたら、このような濃い赤の文ばかりになります。なぜなら『マスタード・パイ』ではまだ英語を読み慣れていないことを想定して、情景描写や心象風景のない、最少限の文で物語が進んでいたからです。

　それに対して本書は、薄い赤の「間」の文がずいぶん入った、かなり本格的な小説となっています。英語としては少し難しく感じるかもしれませんが、ぜひ文の緩急を楽しんでみてください。「大切な文がどれか」というのをここで見分けられるようになっておくと、一般の洋書を読む時の大きな武器となるはずです。

　通常の英語の小説では " " で挟まれたセリフのあとに、そのセリフを誰かが「言った（**said**）、聞いた（**asked**）、ささやいた（**whispered**）、叫んだ（**shouted**）」というような文章が続く場合、そのまま文をつなげることになっています。この時、セリフは後ろの文とつながっているため、セリフの最後はピリオドでなく、カンマで終わります（？や！の場合は特に変化せずにつながるだけです）。このページでは次の文がそれにあたります。

"Which room?" the owner asked.

the の頭文字が大文字でないことに注目してください。こういったセリフのあとにくる文はほとんどが読みとばせるものです。これらの文は、会話シーンで誰がどのセリフを言っているか、読者を混乱させないようについています。

> この村落が現在のエヴァーヴィルの基礎となった。しかし、地質学者の調査の結果、スパイグラス山脈からは金銀はおろか、銅や錫さえほとんど採れないことが公表されると、鉄道の話は立ち消えとなり、わずかに敷かれた線路を残して、開発計画は頓挫してしまう。その後、多くの移住者はこの地をあとにしたが、エヴリー湖の周辺にわずかに残った人々を中心に、エヴァーヴィルは今日まで静かな発展を続けてきた。

英語には、日本語の「私」「ぼく」「おれ」などのように、「自分」を表現する言葉がたくさんはありません。老若男女、誰もが「I」です。また、日本語のように年齢や性別によるしゃべり方のちがいもほとんどありません。方言も少ないし、語尾も変化しないので、セリフだけで個性を出すというのはほとんど不可能です。
　たとえば、こんなシーンが日本語で書かれていたとします。

「洋子ちゃん、あしたぼくと一緒に映画にいかない？」
「疲れてるからやだ。山田さん、一人で行ってください」

　このセリフだけで、日本人なら会話している二人について、ずいぶん多くの情報を読み取れるはずです。しゃべり方がこれだけちがうと、どちらのセリフか見失う心配もないでしょう。しかし、同じ会話を英語でするとこうなります。

"Yoko, would you go to the movies with me tomorrow?"
"No, I'm tired. Mr. Yamada, please go by yourself."

　この場合、洋子と山田は性別以外、ほとんどが不明です。性別も、手がかりになるのはお互いの名前だけです。もしそれも取ってしまうと……

"Would you go to the movies with me tomorrow?"
"No, I'm tired. Please go by yourself."

　これでもうこの会話の主は、年齢も性別もぜんぜん分からなくなってしまいます。だから、英語では日本語よりもずっとひんぱんに「誰々が言った」という説明が必要にな

ORIGIN 〜名前の由来〜
さまざまな説が存在するが、確かなことは分かっていない。もっとも有力とされるのは、金の噂で町が賑わった頃、永遠の繁栄を願ってEvervilleと名付けられたという説である（名付け親とされるのはエヴリー湖のほとりに建つホテル「ファイアーウッド・イン」の初代経営者ウィルソン・P・ウィルソン氏）。

りします。これらの文は、脚本でセリフの前に役名が振ってあるのと同じくらいの感覚で用いられているため、むしろ名前だけ見て読みとばす方が自然とさえ言えます。

> 禁断の表現

pp.6-7
The owner frowned and knocked on the door. When there was no answer, he opened it. He was greeted by an ice-cold gust of wind.
"What the...? Mr. Wishbone?"
Wind was blowing in from an open window. The curtains were flapping against the walls madly. The owner ran to the window and poked his head out.
"Mr. Wishbone!?"
The November cold filled the darkness of the parking lot. The only light came from the half moon above. There was no sign of anyone anywhere.
"Oh my God..."

　前ページとは打ってかわって、ここはほとんどが薄い赤の文です。大事なのは「オーナーがドアを開けた」→「誰もいなかった」という二つの文だけです。セリフも出てきますが、このようにひとりごとの場合はテンポをとるために用いられる傾向があります。
　最後のオーナーのセリフ「**Oh my God**」は、アメリカ人にとって、驚いた時に自然に出る言葉です。英語には感情を表現する言葉が豊富にありますが、中でもこういった普段は使われない種類の言葉は、日本語では決して表現できないインパクトを伴った言葉になります。うかつに使うと信用問題に関わったり、凄まじい誤解を生んだりすることがあるのでお勧めしませんが、英語を学ぶなら避けて通れない要素でもあります。そん

1920年代から30年代にかけて、鉱山発掘の中止に伴い、腹を立てた人々が名前にNをつけて「初めから存在しなかった夢の町」としてNevervilleと呼んでいた時期も存在する（この名前は川の名として現在も残っている）。その後、1950年に設立された市議会によって、「イメージが悪い」事を理由に再びEvervilleに戻され、現在に至っている。

な表現はたくさんあるのですが、今回はひとつだけ、特にひんぱんに使われるものを紹介しておきましょう。

　日本語でも足をぶつけた時などに、思わず「くそっ」と言ってしまうことがあります。このまったくの英語訳となるのが「shit」です。意味も使うタイミングも同じですが、決して意識して使わないでください。知っておいて損はありませんが、上品な言葉ではありません。自然に口から出てきたなら仕方ありませんが、日本人が無理に使うと悪意にとられかねません。どうしても強い驚きを英語で表現したい場面に遭遇したら、まずはオーナーと同じ「Oh my（God）」を小さくつぶやくあたりから始めてみましょう。

so と very はどちらが強い

```
pp.8-11
    I was late...
    I was late again...
    (But it wasn't my fault!)
    I'm cold... got to find the cat... so cold...
    (Where am I?)
    I'm a faliure.  I've always been a failure.
    (It was the cat's fault!)
    Got to find the cat...
    (so cold... so cold... so...)
    cold...
```

　このページでは、エドの思考が断片的に浮かんでは消えています。混乱状態で考えがまとまらないエドは、心の中で自分自身とケンカをしているのかもしれません。

　ここで注目してほしいのは、**so** という言葉の使い方です。この言葉はほかの化粧品の

GEOGRAPHY　〜地理〜

大きな山脈の間に位置しているエヴァーヴィルは夏は涼しく、大変に過ごしやすいが、冬は激しい積雪に見舞われる。スパイグラス山脈から降りてくる風がたえず町の上空を吹いていて、雲の流れが速く、一年を通じて空が高い。当初、町の中心部はエヴリー湖を中心とした地域にあったが、台風の季節におけるたび重なる湖の氾濫で、現在、町の中心は湖から10マイルほど西に移動している。

前につけると「とても○○」という意味になります。
　英語にはこのように意味を強調する言葉がたくさんあります。cold を例にとってみるなら、すぐに思いつくだけでも colder、coldest、very cold、really cold、so cold、too cold、damn cold といった風に、実に多彩です。では、いったいどれがどれよりも強いのでしょう？　どういう状況でそれぞれを使うのでしょう？　——もちろん使う人の好みにもよるので、はっきりとした法則性はないのですが、参考までに一般的なイメージをまとめてみました。興味半分ぐらいで目を通してみてください。

【-er】

　何か比べるものがあって、それよりも大きい場合に使うので、「比較」のための言葉だと思われがちですが、実際には「-er than ○○」という形は比喩として用いる方が一般的です。たとえば「colder than winter」といえば「冬よりも寒い」、転じて「とても寒い」となります。○○の中を強烈な単語にすることによって、-est や so よりもずっと強い強調にすることもできます。

　Our house is colder.（冷静。相手を説得している印象）
　Our house is colder than the north pole.（冷静だがかなり強い意思）

【-est】

　おそらくこの中ではいちばん使用頻度が低い形です。「もっとも強い」という最大の強調ですが、どちらかというと-er と同じく、比喩として使われる場合が多い言葉です。日本語でも大げさに表現する場合に「世界一○○だ」というような言い方をしますが、こういった表現はどちらかというとコミカルな印象を伴います。同様に-est も、少し子供っぽい感じのある強調です。

　Our house is the coldest.（断定的で大げさ。コミカルな印象）

町のほぼ中心を南北に走るヴァレーミルズ通りが、旧市街とニュータウンを大まかに分けている。近年、町は湖周辺をリゾート地として再開発する計画（For-Everville Campaign）を立てていて、旧市街の多くの閉鎖店舗の撤去に乗り出しているが、古くからの住民の反対も根強く、計画の進行は遅れている。

【very】

もっとも標準的で特徴のない、使いやすい「強調」です。気軽に使われすぎるため、あまりインパクトはありません。会話の場合は **very** を強く発音すれば少しはインパクトを与えられますが、文章の中ではそれもできないので、どうしても見過ごされがちです。

Our house is very cold.（単に平均よりも寒いという印象）

【really】

相手がこちらの考えを、思ったほど大げさにとらえていないような場合に、「いや、本当にすごいんだよ」という風に、再確認の意味を込めて使います。意外に強い強調力を秘めています。

Our house is really cold.（一番ではないが、相当寒いという印象）

【so】

とても感情的な強調です。「○○でどうしようもない」というような、かなりせっぱ詰まった気分で言っているのが伝わります。一般論ではなく、言っている本人にとって「すごく○○」な場合に使います。

Our house is so cold.（主観的。切実な印象）

【too】

こういった「強調」の表現の中で唯一否定的なニュアンスを含んでいる言葉です。「すごいけどすごすぎる」というマイナスの意味を含んでいます。

Our house is too cold.（限界を超えた印象。**so** に比べると不思議と冷静）

TRAVEL 〜観光〜

観光の中心は、夏はナマズ料理で知られるエヴリー湖、冬はスキー客で賑わうスパイグラス山脈が主となっている。キャンプ施設やスキーロッジの多くは前世紀半ばに建てられたものであるため、歴史を感じさせるものが多いが、一方で老朽化は否めない。そのため、For-Everville Campaignの一環として一大レジャー施設を建設中であり、すでにニュー・エヴァーヴィル・モールをはじめとする一部の施設は稼働を開始している。

Big Fat Cat and the Ghost Avenue

【damn】

先ほど登場した shit と同じ、「禁断の表現」のひとつです。使ってはいけないという前提があるため、「怒り」や「やけくそ」の感情がよく表せます。投げ捨てるような言い方と言っていいかもしれません。

Our house is damn cold. (憤りを伴った、攻撃的な印象。かなりインパクトはあるが、相手の印象はよくない)

「強調」のために使われる単語はほかにもたくさんあります。もっと強く強調する方法もありますが、とりあえずはこれだけ知っておけば十分です。

物語の主軸

物語を動かすのに重要なのは、なんといってもセリフです。セリフが出てくるだけで、物語は生き生きと動き出します。また、セリフが続くと物語のテンポがよくなり、読みやすくなります。本書でも、12 ～ 17 ページまではエドとウィリーの会話を中心にシーンが進んでいます。「セリフと動き」の間に「周りの風景の説明」が入るオーソドックスな形の文章です。こういった場合には前者が「動力源（濃い赤）」、後者が「間（薄い赤）」になるのがふつうです。

ここでは二種類の割合を見るために、一気に色分けしてみましょう。ちょっと長くなりますが、つながりや割合を感じながら、ざっと流し見てください。

p.12
"Son, you're gonna freeze to death if you sleep here," a voice said. It was a soft voice.

ほかの主立った観光ポイントは、隣町と共同で設立されたエヴァーヴィル＝スタンドポイント地域大学の緑あふれる美しいキャンパス、グラスビュー市まで三時間かけてのんびり川下りを楽しむレイク・エヴリー汽船など。変わったところでは、鉱山採掘が空振りに終わったにも関わらず、その失敗の行程を展示したラッシュロー鉱山博物館がある。

Ed moaned. He was cold. His cheek was lying on something hard.
"Son, you really better wake up."
Ed stirred and opened his eyes. His memory was a blur. He didn't know where or when he was.

An old man was standing over him. The man had a long white beard, very old skin, and eyes that reminded Ed of Santa Claus. But it was a little too early for Santa, and Santa definitely didn't dress like this.

p.13

"Son, I don't know what the heck you're doing here, but you better wake up if you don't wanna become a damn Popsicle."

The old man moved slowly, pushing a baby stroller filled with books, magazines, and newspapers. One of the wheels of the stroller was missing. It had been replaced with the lid of a pot.

Ed got up with difficulty. He was lying in a dark, dirty street. The street was lined on both sides with buildings that had been closed for a long time. It was quiet except for the rattle of the old man's stroller.

p.14

"Where am I?" Ed said in a weak voice. His head was hurting like crazy.

"You don't know where you are?"

"I think... I... I'm lost..."

"Damn right you are. Everyone who comes here is lost. Pretty badly lost, as a matter of fact."

Ed looked around again. The moon overhead cast shadows into every corner. A gust of wind blew down the street.

Ed just wanted to sleep. He didn't want to walk anymore. He had never been so tired in his whole life.

p.16

The old man walked over to a giant pile of junk by the side of the road. The pile was made of stuff that had been thrown away when the street was still a part of the town.

"People have forgotten about this place. They call it 'Ghost Avenue'

Everville's Favorite!

GET A <u>FREE</u> COFFEE ROLL at

THE CORNER CAFE

Located in the Food Court of the New Everville Mall

Nov.11 - Dec.10

Coupon!! with any purchase of over $2

now. We're just ghosts to them."
　The old man picked a long piece of cloth that had probably been a curtain some decades ago. He turned around to Ed and smiled.
　"We call it 'Treasure Island'."
p.17
　Ed blinked. His blurry mind figured out that he was somewhere on the northwest side of town, near the old mines. The area had been busy during the twenties and thirties because of the mining business. The barber from the shop next to Pie Heaven had told him that there used to be a beautiful old cinema here.
　"Folks around here call me Willy. Professor Willy. Because I'm the only one who can read," the old man said.
　He handed Ed the long piece of cloth. Ed took it reluctantly and wrapped it around himself. It smelled bad.
　"I... I'm Ed," he managed to say.
　The light of the moon played with the shadows. It was as if the street was alive.
　"Nice to meet you, Ed. Now follow me," Willy said, and started down the street.
　Ed followed Willy slowly, walking deeper into the darkness of the street.

濃い赤と薄い赤で半分半分ぐらいでしょうか。試しに濃い赤の部分だけを抜き出して読んでみましょう。

　　"Son, you're gonna freeze to death if you sleep here,"
　　"Son, you really better wake up."
　　An old man was standing over him.
　　"Son, I don't know what the heck you're doing here, but you better wake up if you don't wanna become a damn Popsicle."
　　"Where am I?"
　　"You don't know where you are?"

Jeremy Lightfoot Jr.'s
Words of Wisdom

"There are only two kinds of people. Me, and everyone else."

"I think... I... I'm lost..."

"Damn right you are. Everyone who comes here is lost. Pretty badly lost, as a matter of fact."

The old man walked over to a giant pile of junk by the side of the road.

"People have forgotten about this place. They call it 'Ghost Avenue' now. We're just ghosts to them."

The old man picked a long piece of cloth

"We call it 'Treasure Island'."

"Folks around here call me Willy. Professor Willy. Because I'm the only one who can read,"

He handed Ed the long piece of cloth. Ed took it reluctantly and wrapped it around himself.

"I... I'm Ed,"

"Nice to meet you, Ed. Now follow me,"

Ed followed Willy slowly,

　かなりシンプルになってしまいましたが、内容を理解するだけならこれで十分です。本文の脚本バージョンだと言ってもいいかもしれません。

　しかし、これだけではつまらないので、実際の本文では薄い赤の部分が加わっています。全部を読めるなら、もちろんそれに越したことはありませんが、もし難しすぎる文にあたったら、濃い赤の部分を物語の主軸として読みながら、ところどころ薄い赤の文の意味を拾って、頭の中で雰囲気を楽しむことができれば、それで十分です。

Big Fat Cat and the Ghost Avenue

物語にしか使われない言葉

pp.18-19
Meanwhile, in another part of town...
And back in Ghost Avenue...

日本語にも、物語でしか使われない言い回しがけっこうあります。「昔むかし」「その時」「その頃」「一方」「幸せに暮らしました」などなど……これらの言い回しは、日常ではまず使われません。物語専用の表現です。英語にも物語専用の表現というのはけっこうあります。この二つの文も、場面が変わる時に典型的に用いられるものです。

このような物語専用の表現をひととおり知っておくと、話を見失いそうな時に役に立ちます。特に絵本や児童文学ではよく見かけるので、見つけた時にはニヤッとしてみてください。

物語でよく見かける表現一覧

Elsewhere
（A から B へ舞台が移った時に使う）

Meanwhile
（A から B へ舞台が移って、同時に起きている出来事を見せる時に使う）

In another time
（SF やファンタジーの始まりなどで、別世界の物語の冒頭に使う）

Far, far away
（やはり SF やファンタジーの物語の冒頭に使う。宇宙の彼方をイメージさせる）

Once upon a time
（日本語で「昔むかし」にあたる表現。おとぎ話の冒頭の常套句）

A long time ago
(やはり昔話の冒頭に使う。once upon a time よりいくぶん現実的)
happily ever after
(おとぎ話の最後の常套句。日本語では「めでたしめでたし」)
In the end
(最終的な結論の前に登場する置き言葉)
And back (in/to)...
(テレビのニュースでスタジオに戻る時などに使う)

Ghost Avenue とはどんな「道」か？

　さて、本文に戻る前に、エドがたどり着いた **Ghost Avenue** という場所について少し見ていきましょう。もちろん、これは本当の名前ではなく、さびれきった通りの外観からつけられた俗称です。**ghost** というのは一般的に「お化け」のことですが、広い意味では「残像」のようなあいまいな意味も持っています。
　avenue は「通り」を指す言葉ですが、日本人になじみ深いのは **street** の方だと思います。**street** と **avenue** のちがいは微妙ですが、**street** が一般的な「通り」の呼び名であるのに対して、**avenue** は比較的大きな通りに使われるイメージがあります。加えて、**street** や **avenue** は街の道路という印象が強く、田舎の道路にはたいてい **road** という言葉が使われます。さらに細い畦道などは **path** と呼ばれています。
　言葉の説明だけでは分かりにくいと思いますので、それぞれのイメージをイラストで表現してみました。あくまで大まかなイメージです。

Ed's easy to learn Cooking Kitchen
TODAY'S RECIPE
Pumpkin Pie

Big Fat Cat and the Ghost Avenue

path　　　road　　　street　　　avenue

　アメリカの田舎町では、**Ghost Avenue** のように、かつては繁華街だったのに、時代に忘れ去られて廃墟と化している地区をよく見かけます。土地の少ない日本ならすぐに取り壊されてしまうところですが、アメリカでは取り壊しにかかる費用を考えれば、新たに別の地に作り直した方が安上がりだからです。こういった地区の多くは、ほかに行き場のない人々の住みかと化し、やがては治安の悪いスラム街になってしまいます。

　30 年ぐらい前のある日から時が止まってしまったような、これらの街道は実に不思議な雰囲気を持っています。はるか昔に消えた商品を「新発売」と紹介するポスターが壁に残り、あちこちのショーウィンドウに二世代前の人気商品がほこりまみれで飾られています。日中は限りなく無人に近く、世界が滅んだ後のような寂しさがあたり一帯に広がっていて、なんとも言えない気分になります。

ウィリーたちの日常会話

　旧エヴァーヴィル劇場に舞台を移動して、物語もいよいよ後半に入りました。ここからはエドとウィリーの会話に注目していきましょう。『ビッグ・ファット・キャットとゴースト・アベニュー』に出てくる会話は、今までの **BFC BOOKS** よりも現実に近いものです。そのため、砕けた表現や分かりにくい表現も出てきますが、意味が分からなくて

Ingredients
(for the crust)
150g graham crackers
2 tablespoons soft brown sugar
1/3 cup melted butter or
　margarine

(for the filling)
400g frozen pumpkin
1/2 cup soft brown sugar
2 tablespoons granulated sugar
2 eggs
1/2 cup milk

1/4 teaspoon salt
1 teaspoon cinnamon
1/4 teaspoon ginger
1/4 teaspoon nutmeg
1/4 teaspoon clove

も、英語力が足りないからだとは考えないでください。会話の意味が分からないのは多くの場合、英語が分からないためではないからです。
　たとえばアメリカの典型的な若者に何か約束をしてほしいと頼む場合、教科書ではこういう会話になるはずです。

"Please promise me you will come tomorrow."
"Sure, I promise."

でも、この会話が実際に聞けるのは英会話教室ぐらいです。最低でも以下ぐらいのアレンジをされて使われるのがふつうです。

"Promise me you'll come tomorrow."
"Sure."

そして仲のよい若者同士だと、こんな会話になります。

"Tomorrow. Word?"
"Word."

こうなるともはや英語の問題ではありません。word という言葉を辞書で引いても、このセリフの意味はさっぱり分かりません。しかし、実際にこの言い回しを使っている人と話をして、その時の状況や相手の表情、ジェスチャーを見たら、どういう意味かはすぐに分かります。
　地方、年齢、性別などによって、言葉は面白いほど変化します。学校では無敵の文法

```
1. Crush the graham crackers into crumbs. Mix the soft
   brown sugar and melted butter into the crackers and mix
   well. Spread in pie dish. Press mixture with fingers until
   thin to form the piecrust.
```

も、会話の前では無力です。会話で大事なのは通じること、面白いことだけです。それこそがコミュニケーションツールとしての言語本来の姿でもあります。さまざまな人のくせや言い回しを吸収し、面白かったものをまね、つまらなかったものを切り捨てていくうちに、徐々に自分の英語が完成していきます。誰の模倣でもない、自分だけの「英語」です。その時を目指して、どんどん会話を経験していってください。わざわざ外国に行く必要はありません。小説も映画も会話の宝庫です。まずはエヴァーヴィルの人々と会話を楽しんでみてください。

　それではウィリーのセリフに焦点を絞って見ていきましょう。ウィリーはエドに比べてずっと特徴的なしゃべり方をするので、きっと戸惑った方も多いのではないでしょうか。ウィリーのセリフはかなり砕けた英語です。ここまでに登場したウィリーのセリフを下にまとめてみました。

省略されているもの
gonna (p.12) は going to、wanna (p.13) は want to のそれぞれ省略形です。速く発音しているので、音がくっついて聞こえています。

強調されているもの
the heck、damn (p.13) などは特に深い意味はなく、強調として使われています。

その他の言い回し
エドを son (p.12) と呼んでいるウィリーですが、もちろん本当の息子ではありません。年配の方が自分より若い男性を親しみを込めてこう呼ぶことがあります。
Popsicle (p.13) はこんな形をしたポピュラーなアイスキャンディーです。

p.20
　"Here we are," Willy said, stopping in front of a unique two-story structure. Ed looked up at the building in wonder. It was a great big building.
　The Old Everville Cinema really was beautiful. The barber had not been kidding. He had not been kidding about the 'old' part either. But

2. Remove the green skin from the frozen pumpkin after defrosting. Mash and strain pumpkin into puree form. Add rest of the ingredients for the filling and mix well.

the cinema still remained beautiful in a strange sort of way.
 "This used to be a great theater back in the fifties, you know. Big screen, great flicks, buttered popcorn... But that was a long time ago. Now it's our home," Willy said as he pushed open the doors of the once-glamorous theater.

　現実の英語の会話でもっともよく出てくる言葉は何かというと、**and** でも **that** でもなく、ある口ぐせです。このページのウィリーのセリフにある、「**you know**」という慣用句がそれです。直訳したなら「分かるだろ」という意味になりますが、単独でセリフの間に挟まれて出てくる時は、ほとんど意味はありません。

　これは言葉に詰まった時に、アメリカの多くの人が口にする置き言葉のようなものです。映画俳優のインタビューなどを注意深く聞いていると、時々ぽつんと入るのが分かります。緊張している時などは回数が増えるので、相手の気持ちを察するひとつの目安になるかもしれません。

緊張していないエド：
 I think my blueberry pie is really delicious and I'm proud to have made it.

とても緊張しているエド：
 Uh... you know... I think my blueberry pie is... you know, really delicious, and... umm... I'm... you know, proud to have made it.

3. Preheat oven to 200°C. Pour filling into piecrust and bake 45 minutes. (**CAUTION :** The piecrust can burn easily. Wrap the crust edges in foil if necessary.) Cool in refrigerator. Serve with whipped cream.

Big Fat Cat and the Ghost Avenue

もしも状況が分からなくなったら

　ここからしばらくは映画館の中の様子が説明されています。しかしこういったシーンは難しければ無視してしまっても、物語に大きな影響はありません。挿絵を参考にすればどんな状況かはすぐに分かると思いますが、挿絵のない本でも、重要そうな言葉を抜き出していくだけで、頭の中にだいたいの様子を組み立てることができます。

> p.21
> 　Inside, the theater lobby was ruined. The refreshment stand, the ticket booth, and the waiting area had been torn down, and everything had been replaced with piles of cardboard and miscellaneous junk. A few people were sitting there in the dark. The only light inside was a lantern hung from the remains of a chandelier.
> 　A man rummaging through a pile of soda cans looked up and grinned at Ed.
> 　"That's Frank," Willy said as he pushed his stroller through the mess. "He won't hurt you. Nice guy. Stinks, but a nice guy anyway."
> 　"Howdy," Frank said to Ed, raising his hand awkwardly. He had no teeth. Ed just kept walking.

　このシーンで最小限、把握しておく必要があるのは「ruined」「torn down（壊れている）」「dark（暗い）」などの全体の大まかな印象と、「cardboard（ダンボール）」「junk（ごみ）」といった小道具のイメージぐらいです。これらの単語のイメージを空っぽの部屋の中にあてはめてみます。こんな感じになるでしょうか。

このくらい分かっていれば、ストーリーを読むために必要な舞台イメージとしては十分です。

そのあと、次のシーンでは映画館の中心に話が移って、そちらの舞台設定が登場します。

p.22
　Willy walked across the lobby to a set of swinging doors that were hidden behind a broken vending machine. Ed followed cautiously, glancing around the whole time.
　The main part of the theater was better preserved than the lobby, except for one major difference. There was a big hole in the ceiling. The blue half moon shined through the hole, providing a soft light. There was also a warm red glow from a small campfire that was burning directly underneath the hole.

前半はロビー周辺の様子です。もう一度イメージを拾ってみましょう。全体としては「**lobby**（ロビー）」、細かい小道具としては「**swinging doors**（押し開ける扉）」「**broken vending machine**」などがあります。前のシーンのボロボロの部屋にこれらを加えて想像すれば、きっとこんな感じになります。

ミステリー小説で密室殺人でも説明しているのでない限り、舞台説明の多くは「間」のためにあるもので、そういう部分で辞書を引いたり、考え込んだりしていると、舞台

説明のもっとも大切な役割である「物語のテンポの調整」がかえって犠牲になってしまいます。辞書を引くことは決して悪いことではありません。でも、それで全体を見失ってしまったら意味がありません。

　舞台の設定は、漠然としたイメージで十分です。もし分からないところがあれば、そこは想像で埋めてしまってもかまいません。それこそ、映像のないメディアである小説を読むことの醍醐味なのですから。

物語の緩急

　長いシーンは途中で疲れてしまうこともあると思いますが、長くなればなるほど、重要な部分と、「間」の部分とがはっきり分かれてきます。「間」の部分は音楽の間奏のようなものです。今回もっとも長く、物語の中心でもあるシーンを追いながら、文章の緩急について見ていきましょう。エドとウィリーがたき火の端で会話をしているシーンです。

> p.24
> "Here. Use them."
> Willy pointed to a row of seats near the campfire. Ed sat down. He found the seats very mushy, but he didn't care. The seats were much better than the cold street outside.
> "Well, you've met Frank, and that's George and Beejees. Louie's in that box over there, I don't know where Paddy is, but Marv's probably in the basement. He almost never comes out."
> Ed nodded.

最初の部分は完全に薄い赤です。セリフなども入っていますが、ここはまだ導入部分に過ぎないので、軽く読みとばしながら先に進んでしまってもかまいません。

p.25
"What do you do for a living, Ed?" Willy asked as he tossed a few crumpled-up pieces of newspaper into the fire.
"I bake... I used to bake pies," Ed said, staring into the burning fire.
"That's a nice job."
"I lost my shop yesterday. I'm not a baker anymore."
"Sure you are. You're just a baker without a shop."

p.26
"Not just my shop. I lost my house, my savings, my bag, my whole life... all I have left is this."
Ed took his rolling pin out of his coat pocket. Somebody had found it lying near him in the parking lot of the New Mall. It always seemed to survive somehow. Ed tossed it on the ground.
It rolled straight toward the fire. It would have burned up if Willy hadn't reached out and grabbed it.
"Don't. This is important to you."
"No," Ed said. "I'm really not much of a baker. I just like baking pies. I was a mediocre salesman until last year. I quit my job, thinking I could become a pie baker because my mom used to bake great pies. She won a lot of contests. I thought maybe I was like her. But I wasn't. Stupid."

小さな「間」となる薄い赤の文もところどころに混ざっていますが、重要な会話が続きます。エドもウィリーもほとんど動いていないので、基本的に大事なのはすべてセリフです。セリフの多いシーンは重要な部分になることがよくあります。セリフ中心にしっかり読んでみてください。

The Match Prince

BEDTIME STORIES
from the Astyore Library

Willy stood by the fire, listening with a faint smile on his face. It was a smile worn by time and hardened, almost petrified, by the burdens of life.

Ed continued to speak, the light of the fire playing on his face.

"Mom always told me that life was like a blueberry pie. Sometimes it's sour but most of the time it's sweet. She said the most wonderful thing in life was to eat a good, warm slice of pie."

A tear formed at the corner of Ed's eye and rolled down his cheek.

p.29

"But she was wrong, you know. She died of a heart attack when I was in high school. From overwork. My father had left us the year before, and she'd had to work two jobs to raise me. One day when I came home from school, there was a slice of warm blueberry pie on the table. She was sitting in front of the oven, waiting for the pie to cool. But... she wasn't breathing. No last words. I never even said 'thank you' to her. I was too late. I'm always too damn late."

エドの話が核心に近づくにつれて、セリフが長くなり、重要度も上がっていきます。薄い赤の文はどんどん少なくなっていって……ついには消えてしまいます。

Willy walked up to Ed and held the rolling pin out to him. Ed shook his head, tears streaming down his face.

"No. I'm not going to bake any more pies. Life isn't a blueberry pie. A child can see that. It's... it's... more like a mustard pie."

"Look, Ed. You're going to get a good night's sleep, and then in the morning, you're going to go back to your life. You are not one of us. You have a life. Go back to it."

"You don't understand. I can't bake pies like my mother. I don't have it in me. I was only pretending I could."

"That's because you have no idea what a pie is really made of."

The Match Prince

Once upon a time, there was a land of matches. The match people lived there. Water was more valuable than money in the Match Kingdom, because their heads would ignite easily. If they became angry, their heads got hot and burst into fire. If they caught a cold and developed a fever, their heads would heat up and burst into fire. So water was always kept near.

1

ignite＝引火する　burst into fire＝炎を吹き出す　cold＝風邪　develop＝発展する　fever＝熱

"Sure I do. I use the same things my mother did. I even use the same brand of flour. It doesn't make any difference."
"You had a great mom. She understood life well. She knew why pies were important. That's why she was a great baker."
"Pies are just pies. They're not important."

会話が核心に入って、薄い赤の文は完全に消えてしまいました。重要なシーンはゆっくり読むことも大事ですが、テンポを失ってしまわないことも同様に大切です。読む速度はみんなちがうので、自分が飽きない速度で読めば、それが最良です。読んでいて苦痛になるなら、読み込みすぎているのかもしれません。たとえ英語でも、本を読む時はあくまで「物語を読む」のが最大の目的です。「英語」を読もうとすると、物語が頭に入らず、楽しむこともできません。また、文面だけで読んだ英語は記憶に残りません。でも、物語を楽しく読んでいれば、英語は自然に頭に入ってきます。そして、物語と共にいつまでも残ります。

pp.30-31
A long silent moment passed. Ed looked away while Willy tended the fire. The crackling sounds of the fire eating into the wood filled the air. Finally, Willy spoke. His voice was slow and calm.
"Most of us haven't had a slice of pie in years, Ed."
Ed stopped wiping his tears. Still wearing that faint and petrified smile, Willy continued, "Take Frank for example. He's been here for more than ten years now. He's probably forgotten what a pie looks like."
Willy gestured toward Frank, who was now near the campfire, looking for something in another big pile of junk.

まくしたてるようなエドの話のあと、しばし沈黙があたりを包みます。パチパチと燃え

The Match Prince

There was a big lake in the Match Kingdom so water was always plenty. But things changed. The good king Matchionne died of the flu, and Karl Matches became the next king. Karl Matches was a greedy match. He built a watergate around the lake and decided to sell water at a high rate. Soon, the river in the Match Kingdom stopped flowing.

2

flu＝流感　greedy＝欲張りな　rate＝価格　flowing＝流れる

散る薪の音が会話の間の静けさの役目を果たしています。これらの文も詳細に理解する必要はありません。細かい文法よりも、雰囲気を感じることの方がずっと重要です。

たとえば、三文目にたき火の様子が描かれていますが、その表現は「**fire** が **wood** を **eating** している」というものです。少し奇妙に映るかもしれませんが、雰囲気のある表現です。こういう変わった表現はシーンの雰囲気と共に覚えておいてください。どんな雰囲気の時に使う表現か分かることが、物語で英語を学ぶことの大きなメリットです。例文だけではそこまでは分かりません。

pp.31-32

"Why doesn't he just buy one?" Ed said with a rather guilty look on his face. "I mean, he could get a job, couldn't he? A pie is just a buck or so. Frank chose to be here... just like me. Bad luck, but it's probably his own fault. Anybody can buy a piece of pie. You just need to go out and..."

At that moment, Frank moved toward the fire. Ed suddenly noticed that he had no legs.

The tears came back all at once. Ed's face turned red and he covered his mouth with his hand. The tears streamed over his hand.

"I'm... I'm sorry. I didn't mean... oh no... I'm... I'm so sorry. I'm so confused... I'm really, really sorry..."

"No harm done, Ed," Willy said. "Frank was born on the street. Never knew his parents... A car hit him when he was twenty. Three hospitals refused to treat him and he ended up here."

セリフもそうです。エドをここまで追って来た方はみんなエドの性格をよく知っていると思います。これはとても重要なことです。日本語ほどでないにしろ、英語にも人によって言い方に差があります。いかつい顔のプロレスラーが「そうね。素敵ね」としゃべったら変です（面白いかもしれませんが）。やはり「そうだな。最高だぜ」の方が自然

The Match Prince

Young prince, Karl Matches the 2nd, who sometimes secretly went to the city, was not like his father. He was a good match who loved his kingdom. He tried to persuade his father, but King Matches wouldn't listen. Meanwhile, a bad flu was growing in the city and all the match children began to get hot heads. They were going to burst into fire at any time.

3

secretly＝秘密裏に　persuade＝説得する

です。BFCのキャラクターには、あえてそれぞれのタイプの人が典型的に用いるしゃべり方を使ってもらっています。エドは気弱で優しく、ジェレミーは少し高慢な口調に、ウィリーは穏やかな老人のしゃべり方です。

pp.32-33

The soft light of the moon enveloped the theater in its warm glow. The smoke from the campfire rose through the hole in the ceiling, up toward the sky, where it scattered among the clouds. The whole theater seemed like a gentle shelter for life.

"Ed... most of us here will die without eating another piece of pie... and we're the luckier ones. Some people never have the chance to eat pie. Not once in their lives. Some people have never had anything sweet, not in their mouths or in their hearts. For those people, Ed, life isn't a blueberry pie or a mustard pie. Life is just hell."

Willy put the rolling pin down on the seat beside Ed and turned toward the campfire again.

"Sleep, Ed. Then go back. Bake more pies."

シーンの速度が終盤に向かって落ちていくに従って、真っ赤だったページにも、薄い赤の文が増えていきます。読みながら一緒に緊張感をゆるめていきましょう。ちょっとぐらい読みとばしてもだいじょうぶです。でも、**BFC BOOKS** を通して出現する「ブルーベリー・パイ」や「マスタード・パイ」といった、物語のキーワードになっているフレーズが目についたら、そこの文だけはしっかり読んでおいてください。

p.34

And it was a long night. The longest night of Ed's life. He was as tired as possible, but he still could not sleep.
He watched the campfire burn down.

The Match Prince

Prince Karl knew he had to destroy the watergate. But the watergate was guarded by many soldier matches and he would never be able to bring a weapon near it. He needed something to destroy the gate. But how? The children were almost on fire. Mothers were crying in despair. Prince Karl knew there was only one way. He went to the watergate. The guards let him in after they checked for weapons. They found none.

4

guarded＝守られる　soldier＝兵士　weapon＝武器　despair＝絶望

He watched the moon shining in the sky.
And he watched the "ghosts" of Everville sleeping in their beds of garbage. Garbage that he might have thrown away.
He thought about all the pies he had baked. He thought even more abolut the many pies he had thrown away.

p.35
He thought of his mother.
He thought of his mother a lot that night.
Life is like a blueberry pie, Eddie. Sometimes it's sour, but most of the time, it's sweet.
For the first time in ten years, **Ed remembered that there was something after those words.** Perhaps the most important part which he had forgotten a long time ago.
And you know what, Eddie? It's always sweet if you eat it with the people you love.
Ed cried himself to sleep, and in the morning, he knew what he had to do.

映画ならカメラがエドから徐々に引いていくところです。次第に薄い赤の情景描写が増えて、最後にシーンを濃い赤の文が締めくくります。イタリックの文はとても大事なところです。イタリックのセリフなら、その部分はキャラクターが特に大きな声でしゃべっていると思って読んでみてください。ナレーションの部分がイタリックなら、映画をイメージして、エコーがかかった声でナレーションを聞いてみてください。

ひとつのシーンの中でも、このように大事なところとそうでないところが混在しています。それはそのまま、シーンの中の時間の経過を生んでいます。二つのセリフの間に少し「間」をおいて読んでほしいと作者が思っても、「しばし沈黙が流れた」と書くだけでは、その文を読む間しか読者は止まってはくれません。これは無理もないことです。何

The Match Prince

Prince Karl approached the gate. He thought about the suffering town. He thought about his selfish father. He was mad. He was really mad. Prince Karl raised his hands toward the castle and shouted "Father!!" and his head burst into flame. The fire caught on to the watergate and the gate broke open. The water attacked Karl Matches' castle by the lake and destroyed it. The matches were saved, but Prince Karl never returned.

The End

suffering＝苦しむ selfish＝自分勝手な

しろ時間というのはもっとも想像しにくい「もの」です。そのため、情景描写や話の脱線で、実際にそこを読む時間を多くして、物理的に読む速度を遅くしなければなりません。

こういった「間」の部分が「大事でない」と書くことは本当はまちがいです。大事でないところなんて、もちろんありません。でも、より大事なところはあります。

本を最初に読む時は、まず大意をとるつもりで読んでください。小さなことは見逃してもだいじょうぶです。その方が二度目に読む時、きっと楽しみが増えますから。

ニュアンスの宝探し

1. 小さな発見

物語も終盤に入りました。ストーリーの「動力源」となる濃い赤の文と、「間」となる薄い赤の文についてはもう十分説明したと思います。やりすぎてしまわないうちに切り上げて、残りのシーンは宝探し気分で、英語の面白い表現を見つけることにしましょう。一見ふつうの文章の中にも、面白いニュアンスを隠し持っている言葉や表現がたくさん潜んでいます。これらを探すのは、同じ本を二度目に読む時の楽しみだと言ってもいいかもしれません。

> pp.36-39
> When Willy woke up that morning, he couldn't believe what he smelled. It was the smell of fresh-baked pie. It was something he hadn't smelled for a long, long time. Willy got up and found his fellow ghosts standing around the campfire with Ed.
> Ed was slicing up an apple pie.
> "I'll be darned," Willy mumbled, his eyes wide with astonishment.
> A metal container was hanging over the campfire, and more pies

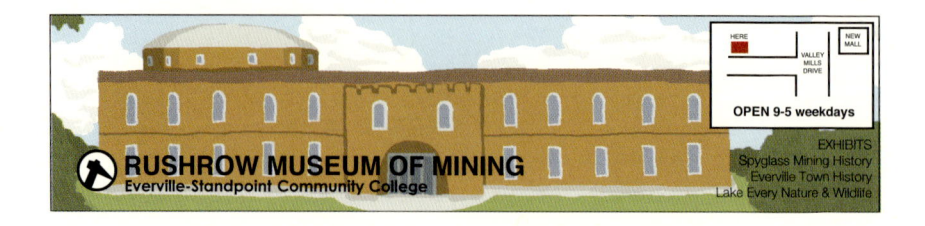

RUSHROW MUSEUM OF MINING
Everville-Standpoint Community College

HERE / VALLEY MILLS DRIVE / NEW MALL
OPEN 9-5 weekdays
EXHIBITS
Spyglass Mining History
Everville Town History
Lake Every Nature & Wildlife

were baking inside of it. Ed saw Willy and spoke to him with a smile.
"I only had enough money for apple jam, so I guess it's not a genuine apple pie. And the crust is just graham crackers. But I did the best I could. I saved you a big piece. Here."
Willy took the slice of apple pie from Ed. It was on a piece of wax paper. No fork, no napkin, but it was really apple pie.
"You were right. I guess I am a baker after all," Ed said.
Willy bit into the pie. It was sweet. It smelled of a long time ago.
"Thank you," Willy said with a big smile.
Ed smiled back and said, "I'm going to get some more wax paper."
"Sure. Oh, Paddy's probably out in front of the theater sweeping. Please give him a slice too."
"Okay, I'll look for him," Ed said, and stepped out of the theater.

日本ではケーキのお店で「アップルパイ」と注文したら、一人分にカットされたアップルパイが出てくるのがふつうです。でも、アメリカで「アップルパイ」と注文したら、巨大なアップルパイが丸ごと出てきてしまいます。このシーンをよく見ると、「パイ全体」を表す時は「an apple pie」となっていますが、「パイ一切れ」を表す時は「a slice of apple pie」というように細かく使い分けられているのが分かります。

こういった「a 単位 of 品物」のように、「全体」と「一人分」で区別するものは英語には数多くあります。特に食べ物関係は豊富です。a slice of bread、a cup of coffee など、アメリカの食文化に欠かせないものほどその傾向が強いようです。しかし、これはあくまで正確な表記の場合であって、日常ではかなりごちゃ混ぜに使われています。とりあえず、慣れないうちはあまり気にしないでください。

この部分に登場する言葉でもうひとつ面白いのは guess です。もともとこの矢印は「(クイズの答えなどを) 推測する」というような意味で使われています。ところが、会話

Jeremy Lightfoot Jr.'s
Words of Wisdom

"Love is a matter of balance (in your bank account)."

の中ではこの言葉は少しちがう形でよく登場します。

　日本語で先に文章を考えてから、頭の中でそれを英語に翻訳して使おうとすると、「I think ～」で始まる文がたくさんできてしまう傾向があります。これは日本語には「～と思う」という表現がとても多く、その直訳が think になってしまうためです。

　ただ、think は正確には「考える」であって、「思う」という要素を持っていない言葉です。think という動作は頭を抱えて熟考した結果を言うもので、日本語の「～と思う」にある気軽さはまったくありません。とても冷静な響きの言葉です。

　これに対して、日本語の「～と思う」とほぼ同じニュアンスで使われるのが guess です。もちろんまったく同じ意味ではありませんが、「guess」には「～と思う」と同じ柔らかなニュアンスがあります。

2. パズルのように

p.40
But Paddy wasn't there.
Instead, Ed saw a big black man standing by the side of Ghost Avenue. The man's eyes were searching for something. Ed froze, the slice of apple pie held in his hand. He recognized the man from somewhere. The man looked like the bodyguard who had been standing behind the rich man at the New Mall's office. He also looked a lot like the man who had grabbed his bag.
At that moment, the man's eyes met Ed's eyes, and Ed suddenly knew what the man had been searching for.
Because the man had just found it.

　エドがジェレミーのボディーガードと対峙するこのシーンは、今回読むのがもっとも難しいシーンかもしれません。特に上記の部分は代役をひんぱんに使用した、英語特有の

表現がたくさん出現します。このシーンをもしそういった表現なしに書き直したとすれば、こんな文章になります。

> Ed found a black man standing in front of the theater.
> The black man was Jeremy's bodyguard.
> He was looking for Ed.
> The black man found Ed.

でも、ここまで **BFC** のシリーズを読んで来た方なら、もうこういう文章ではつまらなく感じてしまうと思います。『ビッグ・ファット・キャットとゴースト・アベニュー』も最後のシーンとなりましたので、ここでは今までよりもだいぶひねった表現を選びました。ゆっくり見ていきましょう。

まず **black man** が立っている場所ですが、本編では単純に「映画館の前」とは書かれていません。前のシーンが「パディは映画館の前にいる」という文で終わっているため、「**But Paddy wasn't there.**（there＝映画館の前）」でシーンを始めることで、自動的にエドが映画館の前に来ていることを伝えています。

そのあと **black man** がエドを探していること、そして、今エドを見つけたことは、以下の三つの文にわたって説明されます。

> The man's eyes were searching for something.
> At that moment, the man's eyes met Ed's eyes, and Ed suddenly knew what the man had been searching for.
> Because the man had just found it.

最初の文では **black man** が目で **something** を探しているということが語られ、その **something** が何かを告げないまま、二つ目の文でエドと **black man** の視線が合います。

"Would you like to buy a car?" Mark asked me at the cafeteria one afternoon. I had been looking for an inexpensive car since last year, so I immediately said "Sure." Mark continued. "I have a friend that wants to sell his car really cheap." "That's great." "There's one little problem." "What?" "His girlfriend died in the back seat."

inexpensive＝安い　cheap＝安く

そして、エドはすぐに **black man** が **search** していたのが「何か（**what**）」に気がつきます。

三つ目の文では **something** は **it** になっていますが、やはりそれが何かは明かされていません。ただ、どうやら **black man** はたった今、それを見つけたらしいことが書かれています。もうお分かりかと思いますが、探していた **something** はもちろん今、目が合った「エド」です。

このような文は、漠然とした「もの」でも代役に置き換えることができる英語ならではの表現です。「**black man** が探しているもの」というひどくあいまいなものを、**something** や **what**、または **it** に置き換えることで、こういったパズルのような文を作ることが可能です。

「あれ」「それ」「彼」のような代役をあまり使わない日本語では、この種の表現はくどくなりがちですが、英語ではむしろ歯切れがよくなるので、好んで用いられる傾向があります。最初はややこしく感じられるかもしれませんが、慣れるとパズルを解くような気持ちで楽しめるので、このような表現が出てきたら言葉遊びの感覚で読み解くことに挑戦してみてください。でも、よく分からなかったからといって気にしないでください。もともと分かりにくいように書かれたものなのですから。

3. 英語はどこまで省略できるか

p.41
　　Ed started to turn around, but it was too late. The man seized Ed from behind and slammed him against the outside wall of the theater.
　　"No words," the man whispered to Ed as he held him against the wall.
　　Completely terrified, Ed was unable to speak anyway.
　　"Understand?" the man whispered again.

"She died?" "Yeah. Suicide. She cut her wrist." "God..." "He changed the whole back seat so it's clean." "Then why sell it?" "Well... he said he saw something in the rearview mirror while he was driving." "What?"   "He didn't tell me what he saw. He just wants to sell the car. He said even one grand would be OK. And it's a Mercedes." "One grand for a Mercedes!?"
2

suicide＝自殺　one grand＝1000ドル　Mercedes＝メルセデス・ベンツ

Ed nodded desperately, although he could not understand what was happening at all. He could barely breathe.
The giant black man stuffed a piece of paper in Ed's mouth and said just two more words.
"Sign it."
Ed nodded at once. It was the only thing he could do.

　日本語はとても省略しやすい言語です。外国人向けの日本語テキストでも見ない限り、省略されていない形の文章を見る機会がないといってもいいぐらいです。特に日常会話の中での省略は凄まじいものがあります。たとえば「明日、あなたはぼくと一緒に映画に行ってくれますか？」というセリフを言う時、「明日、映画行く？」となってしまうのが日本語です。本当に気心の知れた者同士なら「行く？」でも十分伝わるかもしれません。
　それに対して英語は日本語ほど簡単に省略ができません。でも、まったく省略できないかと言えば、そうでもありません。現にこのページで **black man** は最小限まで言葉を省略したしゃべり方をしています。しかし、英語では **A** の箱の主役を省略すると「命令の文」になってしまうという決まりがあるため、省略すればするほど高圧的、または逆になれなれしい文になってしまいます。だから単純な省略ではなく、「約束する」を「**Word.**」の一語で置き換えるようなスラングが省略形の主流となっています（**68** ページ参照）。ただし、スラングは時代と共に変化するものでもあり、自然に身に付くまで使うことはあまりお勧めできません。

4. 表現の難しい矢印

p.42
　The man let him go. Ed dropped to his knees on the ground, the pie falling from his hand. The man tossed a pen at Ed, and then started walking back to the limousine. Shaking all over, Ed picked up the pen

So I bought the car. At first, the story bothered me a little. While I was driving around, I kept looking into the rearview mirror all the time. But I never saw anything. Two months passed and I started to forget about the mirror. The car was great and I felt sorry for the previous owner. He was probably hallucinating after his lover's shocking death. A year passed, and then two years.

3

bothered＝悩ませる　previous＝以前の　hallucinating＝妄想する

and started signing his name. He couldn't think. He was too scared.
　Before he finished signing his name, the sound of the limousine door rang in his ear. Ed raised his eyes from the ground and saw something that made his blood run cold.
　The man was holding Ed's bag.
　And something was stuffed inside. Something very still.
　Something shaped like a big, fat cat.

　人間の動作は、「jump」や「walk」のように単純なものばかりではありません。時にはどうしてもひとつの単語では表現できない動きというものも出てきます。「つかんでいる人間を放す」「ひざが崩れ落ちる」などは動作自体は簡単なものですが、それを一語で表す矢印がないため、文章で表す時には工夫が必要になります。
　ここではそういった変わった矢印をいくつか紹介しましょう。

　The man let him go. というのは、実際には何をしたかというと、壁に押さえつけていたエドから「手を放してやった」ということです。**let** は「何かをすることを許可する」というちょっと変わった意味の矢印で、ここでは「**him**（エド）」が「**go**」することを **black man** が許可した、という形になっています。これが転じて「放す」という意味になります。**let go** は「手を放す／解放する」という訳でひとまとめに覚えられがちですが、やはり実際の意味を知らずにいると応用が利かないので、ぜひ単語単位で理解する方を選んでください。
　dropped to his knees は全身から力が抜けて、バランスを崩したようにひざまずく様子です。ここで **dropped** したのは「自分」です。**Shaking all over** の **all** は「全身」を表しています。**over** は「すべてにわたって」という付録なので、体中がガタガタと震えている様子を指しています。
　run cold は前についている「役者」が **blood** なので分かりやすいと思いますが、日本

Seven years later, the car engine finally broke down and I decided to sell it. I had completely forgotten about the rearview mirror. I drove to a junkyard and parked the car one final time. I reached over to the passenger's seat to open the glove compartment and accidentally bumped my head into the rearview mirror. "Ouch." I said and looked up.
4

junkyard＝ガラクタ置き場　glove compartment＝助手席の前の小物入れ　bumped＝ぶつける

語で言うと「ぞっとする」時の感覚を表しています。

　このような、確たる単語の存在しない感覚や感情を表す時にどういう表現を使うかで、その言語文化の特性がよく分かります。そしてまた、どんなに距離が離れていても、人種がちがっていても、そこで使われる比喩が似たようなものだと知ると、ちがう国の人間や言葉にももっと親しみがわいてくるのではないでしょうか。

5. 大げさであるように

pp.43-46

The man came back, and set the bag down in front of Ed. Then the man picked up the paper. He checked the signature quickly, and without even a glance at Ed, started back to the limousine.

Ed's heart was bouncing in his chest. He had the urge to throw up but he pushed it back. He remembered thinking that all of his problems were the cat's fault.

"Oh, cat... I'm sorry... I'm so sorry..."

Ed slowly pulled the zipper of the bag open.

"AAAGGGGGHHHHHH!!"

Ed shouted as a very frustrated cat popped out of the bag with a snarl and scratched his face. The cat leaped aside, and almost immediately noticed the piece of pie on the ground. <u>The cat took a giant stretch, and with the grace that only cats possess, approached the pie and started to devour it.</u>

A smile of relief appeared on Ed's face, as he sat down on the sidewalk weakly. The limousine had already driven away. Ed leaned against the wall of the theater and let out a deep breath. He still couldn't understand what that had been all about. It was probably something about the vacant space in the mall, but he didn't care anymore. He was just glad that it was over.

The cat finished the piece of pie and looked up at Ed for more. It

---

I screamed. The mirror had turned sideways. It was now reflecting a part of the back seat I never saw in the mirror until now. A woman covered in red was looking at me with sad, angry eyes. It had been there, lying in the small foot space behind the driver's seat, all these years, watching me in silence.

END

reflecting＝反射する

seemed dissatisfied, maybe because the pie was not blueberry.
　"You understand a lot more than you seem to, don't you, cat?" Ed asked. A weak but sincere smile spread across his face.
　"Blueberry pie is the only pie I still make from my mom's original recipe."
　Ed looked into the cat's eyes. The cat looked back. <u>It was a weird but pleasant moment, there on the sidewalk of a forgotten town. One cat and its owner, just staring at each other awkwardly.</u>
　Then, after a long silent moment, the cat burped.

　もし英語と日本語の最大のちがいは何かと聞かれれば、それは英語は「大げさであること」だと言えるように思います。もちろん構造上のちがいや単語の種類など、ほかにもさまざまなちがいはありますが、日本人が英語を使っていて楽しいと感じるのは、日本語では恥ずかしくて言えないことでも、英語なら気軽に言えるからかもしれません。それが民族性のちがいからくるものなのか、英語が感情のあまり入らない言語だからなのか、はっきりとは分かりませんが、日本語で表現すると大げさな「君を愛している」という言葉も、英語で「I love you.」と言うと、ひどく日常的になるから不思議です。
　本文でアンダーラインが引いてあるところは、英語ならではのオーバーアクションや、大げさな説明が入っているところです。せっかく英語で読むなら、ぜひこういう「英語らしい」部分を楽しんでください。

6. 最後の挑戦

p.47

　"Ugh! That's horrible," Ed laughed.
　The cat made an annoyed face, and started to look for somewhere warm to take a nap. It still seemed hungry. Ed's laughter echoed

down the wide, empty road of Ghost Avenue, up and down, over and below, and on into the first glimpse of the day ahead.
Ed Wishbone knew that the rest of his life had begun.

　このシーンは少し難しい文章で終わります。最後から二番目の文は、三色辞典の色分けを見てもらえば分かりますが、実はおそろしく単純な文です。**80%** がいろんな「場所」の付録になっています（正確には「時間」と「場所」の両方ですが）。

　締めくくりの文は、エドがこの日を、これまでの人生と、残された「rest of his life」の分岐点としてとらえていることを頭に入れて読めば、分かりやすくなると思います。

7. ニュアンスの正体

　どんな文にも前後関係というものがあります。その文が出現した背景というものがあります。いつ、どこで、誰が、なんのためにその文を出現させたのか、文に書いてある内容よりも、むしろそれらの背景を理解する方が本来は大事だと言えるかもしれません。人々が文法という法則まで作って、執拗に文を理解しようとするのは、そこに含まれている小さなニュアンスをきちんと拾いたいからではないでしょうか。

　最後の数ページ、文章表現に隠されたさまざまなニュアンスを見てきましたが、物語を二度目以降に読み返す時には、ぜひこういう小さなニュアンスを気に留めて、「おや？」と思うところがあったら、じっくり考えてみてください。

　そうして、ひとつひとつ英語に秘められたニュアンスを集めていってください。時間はかかります。でも、宝探しのようなものです。隠されたニュアンスを発見するたび、自分の中の英語の宝箱に大事にしまっておけば、宝箱の底が見えなくなる頃、英語自体もきっと宝物になっているはずです。

「読めない」という些細な理由

　今回の解説ではセリフやテンポや間、そして重要度という少し変わった視点で物語を見てきました。ここではすべての文章を色で区別しましたが、これは重要度を知る上でのひとつの目安に過ぎません。どれくらい薄い赤の文があるかを実際に目で見てもらおうと、このようなことをあえてやってみました。「こんなにとばしても物語の意味は分かる」という一言を言いたいために、この解説全部があると言っても過言ではありません。

　本が好きな方ほど、「とばして読む」ということには抵抗を感じるかもしれません。でも、本が好きだからこそ、あえてとばしてでも読んでほしいのです。

　子供時代、たとえ読めない本でも、なんとか読みたい一心から、絵を頼りに、想像だけで物語を組み立てた経験はありませんか？　どんなにまちがえながらでも、どんなにとばしながらでも、いい本というのは不思議に面白さが伝わってきます。そして、少しでも「面白い」と感じたら、きっとまた読み返す日が来ます。本当に隅から隅まで読めるまで、何度でも読み返すことができます。

　でも、「読めない」という些細な理由で読まなければ、その物語に出会うチャンスを永久に失うことになってしまいます。それこそが一番悲しい結果です。

　本のページを開いたら、物語の世界に気持ちを委ねてみてください。物語を楽しんでさえいれば、ふと我に返った時、きっと英語が少し分かるようになっています。

　血の通っていない例文よりも、命を吹き込まれたキャラクターたちを信じてあげてください。エドも猫も、いつも向こうで待っていますよ！

ビッグ・ファット・キャットの
付録

今回の付録はちょっと貴重なものです。
まだゴースト・アベニューに活気があった頃、
映画館の再オープンに合わせて配られた広告が
ラッシュロー鉱山博物館に保管されていました。

ここにはその広告が掲載されている博物館の
パンフレットの1ページを抜き出して収録してあります。

今では廃墟となったゴースト・アベニューの
在りし日の姿が、そこにだけ残っています。
現在の様子と比べて、楽しんでください。

EXHIBITION ROOM A-2
HISTORY OF THE TOWN (20TH CENTURY)

TONIGHT!

JUST OFF
LAKE EVERY DR.
AT DOWNTOWN
SQUARE

GRAND OPENING
FRIDAY, JUN 15th

TWO SHOWS EVERY NIGHT!

Enjoy a gorgeous evening of entertainment at...

ALL-NEW EVERVILLE CINEMA

FULL-COLOR STEREO-SOUND

PULSE-POUNDING SUSPENSE!!

THE FLIGHT TO NOWHERE

PLUS 1 CARTOON FEATURE

starring JOHN GOTHAM and SUSAN FARREN

BOX OFFICE OPENS 5:30 TONIGHT

LATE SHOWS EVERY FRIDAY

CHILDREN UNDER 12 FREE ADMISSION

NEW AND IMPROVED CONCESSION STAND

DRESS AS YOU ARE

Grand Opening Flier, 1962

RUSHROW MUSEUM OF MINING

THE "PALACE" YEARS (1928-1960)

During the "Gold Rush" of Spyglass Mountains, "The Palace" started out as a multi-purpose theater for the workers and families in the surrounding area. It quickly became the center of entertainment and enjoyed more than thirty years of good business.

THE "NEW PALACE" YEARS (1960-1962)

After the damage of the 1960 hurricane, the Palace changed ownership and went under complete renovation. The New Palace was designed for a much younger and pop-cultural audience but failed after only seventeen months. The main reason was the high rise in ticket prices.

THE "EVERVILLE CINEMA" YEARS (1962-1979)

After yet another change in ownership, the New Palace became "Everville Cinema" and survived another decade as a family theater for second-run movies. The theater finally ended its long history in the fall of 1979. Currently, the city of Everville plans to revive the theater as a historical landmark, but the project is still in its early stage of development.

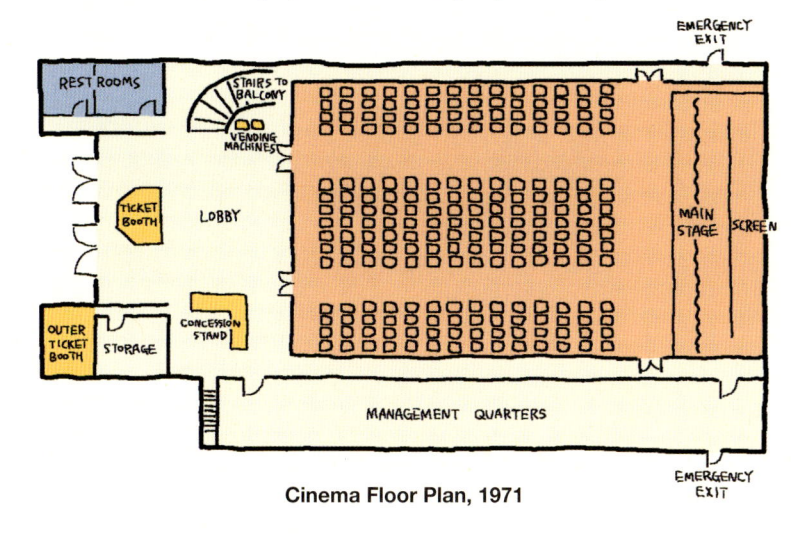

Cinema Floor Plan, 1971

あとがき

　遠くにあるものを目指して歩く時は、途中に小さな目標をいっぱい作っておくとよいといいます。おかげさまでBFC BOOKSも今回、無事三冊目を迎えることができました。まだまだスタッフ一同、毎日が試行錯誤の連続で、一向に要領がよくなりませんが、いろいろな意味で今回の『ビッグ・ファット・キャットとゴースト・アベニュー』はひとつの「区切り」になるのかもしれません。

　エドの人生も、英語の旅も、まだまだ続きます。この物語もまだ終わりではありません。でも、今回の経験で、エドの中の何かが変わろうとしています。それに伴うように、解説の内容も次の段階へと進みました。
　見知らぬ世界。一人で歩いていくしかない世界。怖いのはもちろんですが、進まなければ決してどこにもたどり着きません。まだしばらくここにいてもいいじゃないか、と思う方もいるでしょう。
　でも、不思議なことに、ゆっくりと慎重に進むほど、目標というのは見失いやすくなるようです。大人になると、現実世界の毎日はまるでジェットコースターです。そして、そのジェットコースターの速度にしがみついて生きても、人生で達成できるのはほんのひと握りのことだけです。そう考えると、「少し早いかな」と思う時が前に進む時なのかもしれません。英語を覚えるのが本番なのではなく、英語を覚えて、それを使って世界を広げていく時が本番なのですから。

　でも、今回の『ビッグ・ファット・キャットとゴースト・アベニュー』は、ひとつの区切りにはちがいありません。
　だから、ここまで一緒に来てくださった方はどうか、自分に小さな拍手を送ってあげてください。一年前には英語で物語を読むことなど想像もしなかった方もいると思います。どうかその気持ちを思い出して、「まだまだ英語ができない自分」を叱るよりも、「どうにかここまで来た自分」にささやかな祝福を送ってあげてください。
　英語の旅はまだ続きます。でも、少なくともここまでは来たのです。
　そして、それは素晴らしいことなんです。

Good luck and happy reading!
向山貴彦

　当シリーズは英文法の教科書ではなく、あくまで「英語を読む」ことを最大の目的として作られています。そのため、従来の英文法とはいささか異なる解釈を用いている部分があります。これらの相違は英語に取り組み始めたばかりの方にも親しみやすくするため、あえて取り入れたものです。

STAFF

written and produced by Takahiko Mukoyama	企画・原作・文・解説 向山貴彦
illustrated by Tetsuo Takashima	絵・キャラクターデザイン たかしまてつを
rewritten by Tomoko Yoshimi	文章校正 吉見知子
art direction by Yoji Takemura	アートディレクター 竹村洋司
DTP by Aya Nakamura	DTP 中村文
technical advice by Takako Mukoyama	テクニカルアドバイザー 向山貴子
edited by Masayasu Ishihara Shoji Nagashima Atsushi Hino	編集 石原正康（幻冬舎） 永島賞二（幻冬舎） 日野淳（幻冬舎）
editorial assistance by Daisaku Takeda Kaori Miyayama	編集協力 武田大作 宮山香里
English-language editing by Michael Keezing	英文校正 マイクル・キージング（keezing.communications）
supportive design by Akira Hirakawa Miyuki Matsuda	デザイン協力 平川彰（幻冬舎デザイン室） 松田美由紀（幻冬舎デザイン室）
supervised by Atsuko Mukoyama Yoshihiko Mukoyama	監修 向山淳子（梅光学院大学） 向山義彦（梅光学院大学）
a studio ET CETERA production	製作 スタジオ・エトセトラ
published by GENTOSHA	発行 幻冬舎

special thanks to:

Mac & Jessie Gorham	マック＆ジェシー・ゴーハム
Baiko Gakuin University	梅光学院大学

and a very special thank you to みなみ風

series dedicated to "Fuwa-chan," our one and only special cat

---

BIG FAT CAT オフィシャルウェブサイト
http://www.studioetcetera.com/bigfatcat

幻冬舎ホームページ
http://www.gentosha.co.jp

〈著者紹介〉
向山貴彦　1970年アメリカ・テキサス州生まれ。作家。製作集団スタジオ・エトセトラを創設。デビュー作『童話物語』(幻冬舎文庫)は、ハイ・ファンタジーの傑作として各紙誌から絶賛された。向山淳子氏、たかしまてつを氏との共著『ビッグ・ファット・キャットの世界一簡単な英語の本』は、英語修得のニュー・スタンダードとして注目を浴び、ミリオンセラーとなった。

たかしまてつを　1967年愛知県生まれ。フリーイラストレーターとして、雑誌等で活躍。1999年イタリアのボローニャ国際絵本原画展入選。著書に『ビッグ・ファット・キャットのグリーティング・カード』(幻冬舎文庫)。

ビッグ・ファット・キャットとゴースト・アベニュー
2003年4月5日　第1刷発行
2017年5月1日　第4刷発行

著　者　向山貴彦　たかしまてつを
発行者　見城　徹

発行所　株式会社 幻冬舎
　　　　〒151-0051 東京都渋谷区千駄ヶ谷4-9-7

電話:03(5411)6211(編集)
　　　03(5411)6222(営業)
振替:00120-8-767643
印刷・製本所:株式会社 光邦

検印廃止

万一、落丁乱丁のある場合は送料当社負担でお取替致します。小社宛にお送り下さい。本書の一部あるいは全部を無断で複写複製することは、法律で認められた場合を除き、著作権の侵害となります。定価はカバーに表示してあります。

©TAKAHIKO MUKOYAMA, TETSUO TAKASHIMA, GENTOSHA 2003
Printed in Japan
ISBN 4-344-00319-5 C0095
幻冬舎ホームページアドレス　http://www.gentosha.co.jp/

この本に関するご意見・ご感想をメールでお寄せいただく場合は、comment@gentosha.co.jpまで。